JERUSALEM GATES

JERUSALEM GATES

Kenrick H. Burgess

ELM HILL

A Division of
HarperCollins Christian Publishing

www.elmhillbooks.com

© 2019 Kenrick H. Burgess

Jerusalem Gates

Published in Nashville, Tennessee, by Elm Hill, an imprint of Thomas Nelson. Elm Hill and Thomas Nelson are registered trademarks of HarperCollins Christian Publishing, Inc.

Elm Hill titles may be purchased in bulk for educational, business, fund-raising, or sales promotional use. For information, please e-mail SpecialMarkets@ ThomasNelson.com.

All Scripture quotations, unless otherwise indicated, are taken from the King James Version. Public domain.

Scripture quotations marked NKJV are from the New King James Version˙. © 1982 by Thomas Nelson. Used by permission. All rights reserved.

Library of Congress Cataloging-in-Publication Data

Library of Congress Control Number: 2018954297

ISBN 978-1-595559203
ISBN 978-1-595559142 (eBook)

HB 12.02.2019

DEDICATION

To my daughter Peggy-Ann,

Continue to serve your Lord and Saviour, Jesus Christ. Never Quit. Live your life so that you and your generations to come enter the new Jerusalem, the heavenly city of God.

Your daddy.
Kenrick

My Tribute

In memory of my loving mother Eugenia Leanora Burgess, a pioneer, visionary, virtuous woman of prayer, courage, faith and determination who lived 103 years 7 months and 22 days on planet earth. Her legacy is alive and well.

Eugenia Leanora Burgess
3rd November1913-26th May 2017
*A Woman Who Loved, Who Lived,
Who Fought, Who Conquered*

"An excellent woman, one who is spiritual, capable, intelligent, and virtuous, who is he who can find her? Her value is more precious than jewels, and her worth is far above rubies or pearls. Her children arise up and call her blessed" (Proverbs 31: 10, 25).

Dr Kenrick H. Burgess

CONTENTS

Foreword   ix

Preface   xiii

Acknowledgements   xvii

Chapter One: Jerusalem – the Old City   3

Chapter Two: The Sheep Gate   17

Chapter Three: The Fish Gate   21

Chapter Four: The Old Gate   25

Chapter Five: The Valley Gate   33

Chapter Six: The Dung Gate   41

Chapter Seven: The Fountain Gate   45

Chapter Eight: The Water Gate   51

Chapter Nine: The Horse Gate   61

Chapter Ten: The East Gate   69

Chapter Eleven: The Inspection Gate   75

Chapter Twelve: The Gate of Ephraim   79

Chapter Thirteen: The Prison Gate   83

Chapter Fourteen: The New Jerusalem – the Holy City   91

Chapter Fifteen: Old City to New City   101

There is a God in Heaven

He never sleeps, and He never slumbers.

He changes times and seasons.

He elevates and demotes.

He gives wisdom to men and women.

He reveals deep and secret things.

He is the light of the world.

He is Elohim; the all-wise God.

He is omnipotent, omnipresent, omniscient and infinite.

He is my rock, and there is no unrighteousness in Him.

He is my refuge and my fortress; my God in Him will I trust.

I will always triumph in the works of His hands.

-Kenrick H. Burgess

FOREWORD

The author of this book, my beloved husband Kenrick, has been serving in ministry from his youth. I first met him at one of our church youth camps that was held in Trinidad. He caught my attention because as a young man he was very mature, displayed strong leadership qualities, very humorous and yet very serious about the things of God. We met again when I was a student at the University of the West Indies (UWI); that was when our relationship started and bloomed, and we eventually got married after graduating from UWI. He graduated with a Bachelor of Science with honours in civil engineering, and I graduated with a Bachelor of Science with honours in natural sciences (botany, zoology, and chemistry). Kenrick and I continued to excel academically, educationally, professionally and spiritually.

After teaching secondary-school science in Trinidad and Tobago and in the British Virgin Islands for several years, I pursued and completed a Bachelor of Laws with honours, from the University of London and attended Sir Hugh Wooding Law School, Trinidad, where I attained a Legal Education Certificate to practice as an attorney-at-law in Trinidad and Tobago. I commenced my career in the practise of law as a state attorney and then served as an assistant registrar of the Supreme Court of Trinidad and Tobago. I now have a private practise. I have also authored my first book, *Protecting our Children: The Law, Policy and Procedures for Child Protection in the Caribbean.*

Kenrick is now an ordained minister and volunteer pastor, educator, an expert in project and programme management, a senior and professional civil engineer and an entrepreneur. He is a visionary and has always been in leadership positions wherever he worked or served in the public service, state companies or in his church organisation. His career path led him through the following positions: Ministry of Works in, Tobago, as civil engineer and chief planning engineer. In Trinidad: chief construction engineer, director of highways (Ag), programme director (Ministry of Works); project manager and general manager projects (National Insurance Property Development Company Limited); and Manager, Land Assembly and Construction (National Housing Authority). In the British Virgin Islands he served as chief engineer, public works, in the Ministry of Works. Kenrick has also managed and directed large projects and programmes funded by the Inter-American Development Bank, the World Bank, the European Union, and the Caribbean Development Bank.

I recall the excitement and joy that I felt when we were invited along with other dignitaries, to the *Royal Yacht Britannia*, which was the royal yacht of the British monarch, Her Majesty Queen Elizabeth II. We were introduced to and met with His Royal Highness The Prince Phillip, the Duke of Edinburgh and husband of Her Majesty Queen Elizabeth II. Kenrick was introduced to the duke as her majesty's chief engineer of the British Virgin Islands, and he had the unforgettable honour and pleasure of having a conversation with His Royal Highness The Prince Philip who asked him about the development of the British Virgin Islands.

His Royal Highness The Prince Philip also shared with him his passion for the sustainability of the natural environment of the islands.

In addition to being a highly decorated and successful practising professional, Kenrick has filled several leadership positions in the Wesleyan Holiness Church of the Caribbean. These include chairmanship of various sub-committees, local church youth president, district youth president, district youth camp director, youth area chairman, south-eastern Caribbean; director of leadership training, volunteer pastor, and, on the highest body of our church in the Caribbean, the General Board of Administration, for many years. Kenrick is also a founding member of the Caribbean Graduate School of Theology, Jamaica, and a member of the board of governors from its inception for over thirty years.

Kenrick is a man of one book – the Bible. His sermons and Bible-study sessions have always been insightful and grounded in the Word of God. Hence, it is no wonder that this is such a profound book. My first exposure to the story of the gates of Jerusalem came when he did a series of sermons on the book of Nehemiah for Sunday morning worship and Bible study on Wednesday evenings. There was revelation after revelation, and precept upon precept.

I was very enlightened and inspired as the book of Nehemiah was explained; an otherwise seemingly mundane story of the rebuilding of the wall around Jerusalem came alive and relevant as I recognize that the gates told a story of my life.

Beginning with the Sheep Gate, which represents Jesus Christ as the sacrificial Lamb of God who died for us so that we can have eternal life, it flows with a rhythm, telling the story of God's Plan for humanity.

This is a very enthralling and engrossing book, one which you would not want to put down until you have read it all. It is fantastic that each gate, which on the first appearance seems so ordinary, springs to life upon interpretation and application to one's life. The interpretation of the gates could only have been spiritually discerned. It is indeed a revelation from the Holy Spirit himself, the author of the Word of God.

The chapters are short and crisp, but power-packed. They are gripping! When you start reading this book you are unable to stop, so engaging it is! It is a compelling book that describes the Christian life. The author integrates over four hundred Scripture verses, with the rhythm of the story of the gates, and great hymns at the end of each chapter, bringing them alive and showing their relevance to our daily lives.

Kenrick begins the book with "Jerusalem Now," then "the old Jerusalem – the earthly city of God" and ends with "the new Jerusalem – the heavenly city of God." You will experience reconciliation at the Sheep Gate, the Great Commission at the Fish Gate, consecration and how to live holy in an unholy world at the Old Gate.

You will obtain inspiration for handling temptation, persecution and affliction, receive compensation for what you have been through at the Valley Gate, experience mental elimination of the cluttered mind, concentration and transformation at the Dung Gate, and so much more as you continue the journey through the other gates towards the Inspection Gate.

He concludes with Handel's Hallelujah chorus from the "Messiah." This book is amazing. As you read, you are singing, rejoicing and testifying of the goodness of the Lord and a picture of your life emerges. You are revitalized and rebooted to enter the new Jerusalem. What a fantastic book! Once I started reading it, I could not stop. Thanks, KB! This book is indeed a gift from God.

This book is for your entire family. As you read this book, may you be blessed and motivated to give your life to Jesus Christ as your Lord and Saviour, so that when He comes again, you would be ready to enter the new Jerusalem! Selah.

Margaret J. Burgess.
Attorney-at-Law
Former Assistant Registrar of the Supreme Court,
Trinidad and Tobago.
West Indies

PREFACE

As I studied the book of Nehemiah during the writing of one of the books on biblical project management, I was moved by his journey, his leadership, his prayer life and his legacy. Jerusalem captivated my soul, the sequence, location and the names of the entry and internal gates arrested my heart, and I was overtaken with excitement and passion. The "footprint" shape of the Jerusalem in Nehemiah's time gripped my mind. I followed Nehemiah's footprints and walked around Jerusalem; its gates spoke loudly to me. I was astounded! The gates in the wall around Jerusalem tell a story about the life of the Christian and his destiny. They also speak of those who rejected the gospel. It is a story that I was compelled to share with my generation and the world – the story of the **twelve gates of the old Jerusalem.**

Also, God's Love for Jerusalem **"captured my attention."** The following are recorded in the Scriptures:

"For the LORD has chosen Zion; He has desired it for His dwelling place: This is My resting place forever; Here I will dwell, for I have desired it."[1]

-PSALM 132:13–14, NKJV

*"And it **shall** come to pass that he who is left in Zion and remains in **Jerusalem** will **be called** holy-everyone who is recorded among the living in **Jerusalem.**"*[2]

-ISAIAH 4:3 NKJV

*"At that time **Jerusalem shall be called** The Throne of the Lord, and all the nations **shall be** gathered to it, to the name of the Lord, to **Jerusalem**. No more **shall** they follow the dictates of their evil hearts."*[3]

-JEREMIAH 3:17, NKJV

"Thus says the Lord: 'I will return to Zion, And dwell in the middle of **Jerusalem. Jerusalem shall be called** the City of Truth, The Mountain of the Lord of hosts, The Holy Mountain.'"[4]

-ZECHARIAH 8:3, NKJV

"His foundation is in the holy mountains. The LORD loves the gates of Zion more than all the dwellings of Jacob. Glorious things are spoken of you, O city of God! Selah."[5]

-PSLAM 87:1–2, NKJV

"Awake, awake, put on yourself in your strength, O Zion; Put on yourself in your beautiful garments, O Jerusalem, the holy city"[6] (Isaiah 52:1, NKJV). "Thus, says the LORD of hosts: I am zealous for Zion with great zeal; with great fervour, I am zealous for her. Thus, says the LORD: I will return to Zion, and dwell in the midst of Jerusalem."[7] O What Love!

-ZECHARIAH 8:23, NKJV

This book is divided into three sections. **Part 1** provides insights of Jerusalem, the city of God, its early history, wars, challenges, victories and the views of God on Jerusalem as revealed in the Scriptures. **Part 2** explains the significance and meaning of the twelve gates of the old Jerusalem. **Part 3** concludes with an adventure into the new Jerusalem. The wonder and beauty of the new Jerusalem filled my entire being. There are no words to explain its exquisiteness, loveliness, attractiveness and gorgeousness. Only the omnipotent God could have designed and built such a city, the holy city of God. As you read and study this book, you will experience this extraordinary Jerusalem adventure that will radically change your life. This book is for you. It can change your destiny. You can find God's purpose for your life. May the God of heaven grant you His favour as you read this book.

Kenrick H. Burgess
Author.

In a world of self-righteousness and compromise, the Word of God is an oasis of courage and hope.

-KENRICK H. BURGESS

"Every word of God *is* pure;
    He *is* a shield to those who put their trust in Him."

-PROVERBS 30:5, NKJV

ACKNOWLEDGEMENTS

First, I thank my risen Lord, Jesus Christ, for coming into this world, dying on the cross at Calvary and making eternal life available to me, which I accepted, and now I am saved, and my household. To God be the Glory. I acknowledge that all the insights, revelations, abilities, skills and vision for this book were God-enabled. His Holy Spirit guided and helped me. It was not I, but the Christ, who is living in me and made this book possible.

Secondly, I thank the wife of my youth, Margaret, for her support, love and writing the foreword to this book. Her editing inputs as an attorney-at-law and educator, her analysis and her exhilaration for this work were encouraging and energizing. I acknowledge the support and love of my exceptional daughter Peggy-Ann, and the many others who graciously endorsed and appreciated this book. Thanks.

I thank Professor Andrew Jupiter, Rev. Dr Anthony Oliver, Rev. Dr Shelton Wood and Rev. Whitfield Lawrence for their wonderful endorsements of this book. Special thanks to my publishers for their excellent work.

Thank you all very much.

Kenrick

"Great is the LORD, and greatly to be praised in the city of our God, in the mountain of his holiness.Beautiful for situation, the joy of the whole earth, is mount Zion, on the sides of the north, the city of the great King."

- Psalm 48:1-2

PART 1

JERUSALEM, CITY OF GOD

"Awake, awake; put on thy strength, O Zion; put on thy beautiful garments, O Jerusalem, the holy city."

-ISAIAH 52:1A, KJV

"Zion is called the city of God. '*and they shall call you The City of the LORD, Zion of the Holy One of Israel.*'"

-ISAIAH 60:14, NKJV

"Great is the LORD, and greatly to be praised in the city of our God, in the mountain of his holiness. Beautiful for situation, the joy of the whole earth, is mount Zion, on the sides of the north, the city of the great King."

-PSALM 48:1–2, KJV

CHAPTER ONE

JERUSALEM – THE OLD CITY

"The LORD had said, in Jerusalem shall My name be forever."[8]

-2 CHRONICLES 33:4B, NKJV

Jerusalem, the Focus of the World

It is remarkable that in a world that has approximately 7.6 billion people, the city of Jerusalem, with an area of 0.9 square kilometres (0.35 m²) and a population of roughly 865,700 people, is the focus of attention of the nations of the world in 2019. Jerusalem is situated where Asia, Africa and Europe meet. It is the capital of Israel, located in the Judean Mountains between the Mediterranean Sea and the Dead Sea. The State of **Israel** had a population of approximately 8,793,000 inhabitants at the end of 2017.

Jerusalemites are of varied national, ethnic and religious denominations. These include among others Europeans, Middle Easterners and African Jews; Georgians; Armenians; Muslims; Protestants; Greeks; and Greek Orthodox, Syrian Orthodox, and Coptic Orthodox Arabs. Many of these groups were once immigrants or pilgrims who have over time become near-indigenous populations and claim the importance of Jerusalem to their faith as their reason for moving to and being in the city (Central Bureau of Statistics, December 2013, April 2013, September 2012).

On 6 December 2017, Mr Donald Trump, president of the United States of America (USA), the wealthiest and most militarily powerful nation in the world today, decided to recognize Jerusalem as Israel's capital and to move the embassy of the United States of America to East Jerusalem. President Trump's announcement enraged the Palestinians and thrilled the Jews in West Jerusalem. The Muslim and Arab nations condemned President Trump's independent decision to recognize Jerusalem as Israel's capital and consider it "null and void legally" and an "attack" on the rights of the Palestinian people. They accused the USA of "deliberately undermining" peace efforts and warned that it had given "impetus to extremism and terrorism."

At an emergency session of the United Nations General Assembly on Thursday, 13 December 2017, 128 countries voted in favour of the non-binding resolution to reject President Donald Trump's controversial decision on 6 December 2017. Nine countries voted against, while thirty-five countries abstained. The General Assembly voted during the rare emergency meeting to ask nations not to establish diplomatic missions in the historic city of Jerusalem, and delegates were warned that the decision by the United States of America risked igniting religious wars across the already turbulent Middle East and even beyond.

Additionally, on 13 December 2017, the leaders of fifty-seven Muslim nations called on the world to recognize "the State of Palestine and East Jerusalem as its occupied capital." Notwithstanding, a presidential order was issued in the United States of America on 6 December 2017 to relocate its embassy to East Jerusalem in May 2018.

USA Opening of Embassy

The USA officially opened its embassy in Jerusalem on Monday, 14 May 2018, which was the fifty-first anniversary of the annexation of East Jerusalem during the 1967 Six-Day War. The USA said its decision to relocate its embassy from Tel Aviv to Jerusalem was a "national security priority" and it chose the date to coincide with the seventieth anniversary of Israel's establishment. Tens of thousands of Israelis marched through Jerusalem's old city to mark the day. Many sang, danced and waved Israeli flags. In moving the embassy from Tel Aviv to the holy city, the president of the USA, Mr Donald Trump, said,

> *"For many years, we have failed to acknowledge the obvious, plain reality that the [Israeli] capital is Jerusalem. At my direction, the United States finally and officially recognize Jerusalem as the true capital of Israel."*

At the inauguration ceremony the Israeli prime minister, Mr Benjamin Netanyahu, declared:

"President Trump, by recognizing history, you have made history. This is the day that will be engraved in our collective national memory for generations to come. Today, the embassy of the most powerful nation on earth, our greatest ally, the United States of America, opened here." Netanyahu added that it was a "great day for Israel," for the US-Israel alliance and peace. "We are in Jerusalem, and we are here to stay." Trump's decision recognized a 3,000-year Jewish connection to Jerusalem and the "truth" that Jerusalem would be Israel's capital under any future peace deal. What a glorious day. Remember this moment. "This is history." Netanyahu continued, "You can only build peace on truth, and the truth is that Jerusalem has been and will always be the capital of the Jewish people, the capital of the Jewish state."

The Palestinians, who claim East Jerusalem as the capital of a future state, vehemently oppose the relocation. They protested for weeks before the opening, and violence increased in the hours before the opening ceremony at spots along the Gaza-Israeli border. Palestinian protesters hurled stones at Israeli troops during a protest on the Gaza Strip's border with Israel on Monday, 14 May 2018. At least fifty-eight Palestinians were reported killed by the Gaza Health Ministry. The *BBC World News* and the *Associated Press* reported that fifty-seven Palestinians were killed by gunfire and tear-gas inhalation overcame a baby. Also, 1,360 Palestinians were alleged wounded by gunfire, including 130 who were in serious or critical condition. Many of the allies of the USA, along with its foes, criticized the decision of the USA to open its embassy in Jerusalem, saying it would increase tensions in the Middle East. The United Nations Security Council held an emergency meeting on Tuesday, 15 May 2018, on the violence in Gaza but was unable to reach a consensus.

Jerusalem Sites

Jerusalem is considered a holy city in the three major Abrahamic religions: Judaism, Christianity and Islam. In Sunni Islam, Jerusalem is the third holiest city after Mecca and Medina. The city is also the home to key religious sites sacred to Judaism, Islam and Christianity, among them the Temple Mount with its Western Wall, the Dome of the Rock and the al-Aqsa Mosque and the Church of the Holy Sepulchre. Outside the old city stands the Garden Tomb. Jerusalem is also home to some Israeli non--governmental institutions of national importance, such as the Hebrew University, and the Israel Museum with its Shrine of the Book.

Early History of Jerusalem

Earliest archaeological evidence found the first settlement of Jerusalem in 3500 BC in Gihon Spring, and in 2500 BC the first houses were built in the area. In the middle of the Bronze Age, 1800 BC, there was the construction of the first city wall. At the beginning of the Iron Age in 1200 BC Jerusalem was conquered by Canaanites (Jebusites). Jewish history is centred around Jerusalem from the time of Abraham's gifts to Melchizedek, king of Salem,[9] and throughout the history of the kings of Israel. Jerusalem has a long history of conquests by competing and different powers.

In 1000 BC, David, the most revered king of Israel, captured the city and established it as the capital of Israel, and his son King Solomon built the glorious and first temple[10] in the city. The Babylonians led by King Nebuchadnezzar besieged Jerusalem on at least three occasions. In 605 BC, he occupied the city. In 586 BC, he broke down the walls of Jerusalem, destroyed the temple and burnt the city.

In **556 BC**, King Belshazzar (grandson of King Nebuchadnezzar) ruled until the fateful night of 13 October 556 BC, when the Medes and Persians entered Babylon and captured the city.[11] **Cyrus** the Great established the Persian Empire and ruled from 559–531 BC. He issued the decree that permitted the Jews to return and build their **temple in Jerusalem**. His son Cambyses (529–522 BC) allowed the work on the temple to continue. Darius the Great (520–486 BC) saved the Persian Empire and established law and order after the chaos that followed the death of Cambyses II (529–522 BC). Xerxes I (486–465 BC) was the son of Darius the Great, and the King Ahasuerus who married Esther in the book of Esther. Artaxerxes was the son of King Ahasuerus (Xerxes I) and was on the throne when both Ezra and Nehemiah returned to Jerusalem.[12] He ruled Persia from 465 BC to 423 BC (Wilmington 1984, 227).

In 332 BC, the Greek leader Alexander the Great conquered Judea and Jerusalem and later incorporated it into the Ptolemaic Kingdom (301 BC) and the Seleucid Empire (200 BC). In 63 BC, the Roman general Pompey captured Jerusalem.

In AD 70, Roman forces destroyed Jerusalem and demolished its second temple, and again in AD 135 and rebuilt Jerusalem as a Roman city. In 614, the Persians captured Jerusalem, and in 629 the Byzantine Christians recaptured Jerusalem from the Persians. The first Muslim period began in 638 after Caliph Omar captured Jerusalem between 636–7. It was then ruled between 661 and 750 by the Umayyad Dynasty, and in 691 the Dome of the Rock was built on the site of the destroyed Jewish temples. Between 750–974, Jerusalem was ruled by the Abbasid Dynasty.

In 1099, the first crusaders captured Jerusalem. In 1187, Saladin captured Jerusalem from the crusaders, and between 1229–1244 the crusaders briefly recaptured Jerusalem twice. In 1250, the Muslim caliph dismantled the walls of Jerusalem, and in 1517 the Ottoman Empire captured Jerusalem under Sultan Selim I, who proclaimed himself caliph of the Islamic world. Between 1538 and 1541, Suleiman the Magnificent rebuilt the walls of Jerusalem. In **1917**, the Ottomans were defeated at the Battle of Jerusalem during World War I and the British army took control.

In 1948, the State of Israel was established, and Jerusalem was divided by armistice lines between Israel and Jordan and was accepted as a full member nation of the United Nations.

The 1967 Six-Day War

The Six-Day War took place between 5–10 June 1967 and was the third of the Arab-Israeli wars. Israel captured from Jordan: East Jerusalem, which included Jerusalem's old city and some of the holiest sites of Judaism, Christianity and Islam, such as the Temple Mount, the Western Wall, the al-Aqsa Mosque, the Dome of the Rock, and the Church of the Holy Sepulchre, as well as some adjacent neighbourhoods. East Jerusalem with expanded borders, then came under direct Israeli rule.

During the period of 27–28 June 1967, East Jerusalem was integrated into Jerusalem by extension of its municipal borders and was placed under the law, jurisdiction and administration of the State of Israel. In a unanimous General Assembly resolution, the UN declared the measures were trying to change the status of the city, making it invalid. Nevertheless, Jerusalem was annexed by Israel by the 1980 Jerusalem Law, which refers to Jerusalem as the country's undivided capital, an act that was internationally condemned. All branches of the Israeli government are located in East Jerusalem, including the Knesset (Israel's parliament), the residences of the prime minister and the president, and the Supreme Court.

The world is asking the question today, who owns East Jerusalem? Is it the Palestinians? Is it the Jews? or the Israelites? Alternatively, is it the Palestinians and Jews in a divided City? Hear the Word of the Lord.

Jerusalem, the City of God

Jerusalem is called "the city of our God"[13] and the city of Zion. Zion is called the city of God. *"And they shall call you the city of the LORD, Zion of the Holy One of Israel."*[14] It is where the LORD has dwelt and will dwell again, *"for the LORD dwells in Zion."*[15] It is also the Jews' holy city. It represents the Jewish national identity. It was blessed by God's extraordinary presence in the temple. Jerusalem is not only a historic city, which has for centuries been the centre of the life of the nation of Israel, but it is God's city.

Jerusalem is used in a pictorial sense throughout the Scriptures as the place where God desires to dwell.

"For the LORD has chosen Zion; He has desired it for His dwelling place: This is My resting place forever; Here I will dwell, for I have desired it."[16]

-PSALM 132:13–14, NKJV

*"And it **shall** come to pass that he who is left in Zion and remains in **Jerusalem** will **be called** holy – everyone who is recorded among the living in **Jerusalem.**"*[17]

-ISAIAH 4:3, NKJV

*"At that time **Jerusalem shall be called** The throne of the Lord, and all the nations **shall be** gathered to it, to the name of the Lord, to **Jerusalem**. No more **shall** they follow the dictates of their evil hearts."*[18]

-JEREMIAH 3:17, NKJV

"Thus, says the Lord: 'I will return to Zion and dwell in the midst of **Jerusalem, and it shall be called** the City of Truth, The Mountain of the Lord of hosts, The Holy Mountain.'"[19]

-ZECHARIAH 8:3, NKJV

9

The psalmist declared:

"For the LORD has chosen Zion; he has desired it for His dwelling place: 'This is My resting place forever; here I will dwell, for I have desired it.'"[20] Zechariah affirmed: *"Thus says the Lord: I will return to Zion and dwell in the midst of Jerusalem, Jerusalem shall be called the City of Truth, and the mountain of the Lord of hosts, the holy mountain."*[21]

-ZECHARIAH 8:3, NKJV

"His foundation is in the holy mountains. The LORD loves the gates of Zion more than all the dwellings of Jacob. Glorious things are spoken of you, O city of God! Selah"[22]

-PSALM 87:13, NKJV

The psalmist connected Jerusalem's geography with divine protection:

"As the mountains surround Jerusalem, so the Lord surrounds His people from this time forth and forever."[23]

-PSALM 125:2, NKJV

In **Isaiah 66** all the nations are pictured as bringing sacrifices to *"**My holy mountain Jerusalem**,"* as *declared by the Lord through the prophet Isaiah.* Now, whose report would you believe?

Prophecies about Jerusalem

Jerusalem will be the centre of world events in the end times. The promises regarding the regathering of Israel by the prophet Ezekiel[24] are remarkable.

The prophet Joel prophesied:

"For, behold, in those days, and in that time, when I shall bring again the captivity of Judah and Jerusalem, I will also gather all nations, and will bring them down into the valley of Jehoshaphat, and will plead with them there for my people and for my heritage Israel, whom they have scattered among the nations, and parted my land." [25]

-JOEL 3:1-2, KJV

Jesus prophesied that Jerusalem would be trampled by Gentiles until the times of the Gentiles are fulfilled.[26] Today, what is happening in Jerusalem is God's "critical sign" for us of the end times. We must keep our eyes on Jerusalem.

Nehemiah of Jerusalem

Nehemiah was the cupbearer to the king of Persia. He was an officer of high rank at ancient oriental courts, a person of distinguished merit and loyalty. He was a devout man of prayer and keen foresight. He was courageous. He was resilient. He was determined, and a convincing communicator and strategist. He was also a person of the highest integrity. He was a determined leader.

Nehemiah got a report from his brother about the conditions of the walls, gates and the destruction and despair of Jerusalem, the city of his ancestors. He wanted to bring glory to God and restore the reality and power of God's presence among his people. Inspired by God, he gave up one of the most powerful positions in his day and volunteered to rebuild the wall around Jerusalem. The king gave him the approval to do the project and promoted him to the position of governor of Judah and its province, Jerusalem.[27]

Nehemiah rebuilt the wall around Jerusalem and its gates in **fifty-two** days, then had the city repopulated and led the people into spiritual revival and recovery. When all the enemies of the project heard that the wall was completed in such a brief time, all the surrounding nations were afraid and lost their self-confidence, because they realized that this work had been done with the help of God.[28] **Figure 1** shows a map of Jerusalem in Nehemiah's day, which illustrates the location of the gates.

The Twelve Gates of the Old Jerusalem

The wall that surrounded Jerusalem in Nehemiah's day had ten gates. The gates were: the Sheep Gate, the Fish Gate, the Old Gate, the Valley Gate, the Dung Gate, the Fountain Gate, the Water Gate, the Horse Gate, the East Gate and the Inspection Gate. There were also two other gates, the Ephraim Gate and the Prison Gate, which had their unique meanings. God has within the gates of Jerusalem critical spiritual truths for us today. For example, the order and position of the **gates** are very particular and strategic, and provide an understanding into the journey that God takes each of His children on, as well as the voyage of the church until judgment day.

Enjoy your journey around Jerusalem. Experience the rhythms as you walk towards each gate. Study the map of Jerusalem in Nehemiah's day. Consider the length of the journey between the gates and the strategic location of the temple. Ponder on your experience as you exit each gate. No matter who you are: rich or poor, young or old, Christian or Muslim, Jew or Gentile, the gates around Jerusalem. have a message for you. Ask yourself: What does this gate mean me? How does it apply to my life? You will find meaning, hope, peace, and courage to overcome the struggles of life.

Jerusalem – The Old City

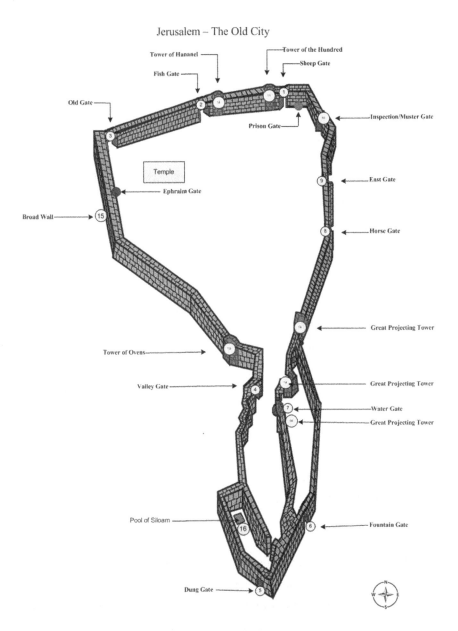

Figure 1: Map of Jerusalem in the time of Nehemiah

The psalmist declared:

"Our feet have been standing within your gates, O Jerusalem."[29]

-PSALM 122:2, KJV

Isaiah the prophet declared:

"Open ye the gates, that the righteous nation which keeps the truth may enter in."[30]

-ISAIAH 26:2, NKJV

The psalmist shouted:

"Enter into his gates with thanksgiving, and into his courts with praise, be thankful unto him; and bless his name, for the LORD, is good; his mercy is everlasting, and his truth endures to all generations."[31]

-PSALM 100:4–5, NKJV

Jesus declared:

"I am the door: by me, if any man enters in, he shall be saved, and shall go in and out, and find pasture."[32]

-JOHN 10:9, KJV

The preservation and focus of Jerusalem through centuries past to the present are not accidents. God has kept the Jews in East Jerusalem for over 3,000 years throughout many wars and battles, and is still keeping Jerusalem today. He has a story to tell the people of every nation in the world about Jerusalem. Let us, therefore, take a walk of faith around the wall of the of Jerusalem, a province of Judah in the time of Nehemiah, and examine each of its twelve gates. You will be blessed.

PART 2

JERUSALEM'S TWELVE GATES

"Lift up your heads, O ye gates; and be ye lifted up ye everlasting doors, and the King of glory shall come in. Who is this King of glory? The LORD strong and mighty, the LORD mighty in battle. Lift up your heads, O ye gates; even lift them up, ye everlasting doors; and the King of glory shall come in. Who is this King of glory? The LORD of hosts, he is the King of glory. Selah."[33]

-PSALM 24:7–10, KJV

CHAPTER TWO

THE SHEEP GATE

"Believe on the Lord Jesus Christ, and you will be saved, you and your household."[34]

-ACTS 16:31, NKJV

The Sheep Gate[35] is the first gate identified in the wall around Jerusalem. It was used for bringing into the city the sheep and lambs used in the temple for sacrifice. Sheep are symbols of sacrifice in Scripture. The gate was near the temple area on the northern wall. The rebuilding of the wall around Jerusalem began from the Sheep Gate. The high priest and his fellow priests built it. The Sheep Gate had no locks or bars, symbolizing that the door of salvation is open to everyone. It was the only gate sanctified, setting it apart as a select gate. It reminds us of Isaiah's great word about Jesus, "as a sheep before her shearers is dumb, so he opened not his mouth."[36] Remember how John the Baptist greeted our Lord with the words, "Behold, the Lamb of God who takes away the sin of the world."[37] The Sheep Gate speaks to us of the cross and the sacrifice that was made for our sins. Jesus' death on the cross is the starting point for Christians.

We are all guilty before God: we have all sinned and have come short of the glory of God; *all we like sheep have gone astray, **everyone to his*** *way*.[38] The whole race of mankind lies under the stain of original sin. We have all gone astray from God our rightful owner, alienated ourselves from God, from what He designed us to move towards and the way he appointed us in which to walk.

We have gone astray like sheep, wandering without hope, struggling to find our way home again. That is our true character; we are bent to regress from God, but altogether unable of ourselves to return to him. We slight God in going astray from him, for we turned aside everyone to his own way, and thereby set up ourselves, and our own will, in competition with God and His will. Instead of walking obediently in God's way, we have turned willfully and stubbornly in our own way, the way of our hearts the way that our appetites and passions led us. We have set up ourselves as our own masters, to do what we want and have what we want, but Jesus Christ "has come to seek and to save that which was lost"[39] (Luke 19:10, KJV).

To find us and to bring us back to himself, the Lord "...laid on Him the iniquity of us all"[40] (Isaiah 53:6, KJV), and further, "...God demonstrated His love towards us, in that while we were still sinners, Christ died for us"[41] (Romans 5:8, KJV). "For God so loved the world that He gave His only begotten Son that whosoever believes in Him should not perish but have everlasting life"[42] (John 33:16, KJV). Jesus said, "I am the door, by me if any man enters in he shall go in and out, and find pasture"[43] (John 10:9, KJV), that is, all the divine resources and provisions that God has prepared for them who love Him. To receive salvation and to enter God's kingdom, everyone must enter through the door. It was Jesus who said, "Truly, truly, I say to you, I am the door of the sheep"[44] (John 10:7, KJV).

When I was a boy, I reflected on God's love and forgiveness, entered the "Sheep Gate," trusted in Christ and accepted His payment for my sins by faith. I always remember the first chorus I learned and sang when I attended my first Inter-School Christian Fellowship (ISCF) meeting when I entered secondary school in Form 1. It goes like this:

Teenagers, are you lonely?
Do you need a friend?
Take Jesus as your Saviour
He will lead you to the end.
He will be your Guide,
Stay by your side,
Teenagers take Jesus today.

I accepted Jesus as my Saviour and Lord. You can do the same today. He is lovely, faithful and true. He has never let me down. The moment you trust Christ, the following delightful things happen to you:

1) All your sins are forgiven;[45]
2) You become a child of God;[46]
3) You receive eternal life;[47]
4) You are delivered from the power of darkness and conveyed into the kingdom of the Son, of His love, in whom we have redemption through His blood, the forgiveness of sins;[48]
5) Christ comes to dwell within you;[49]
6) You become a new creation;[50]
7) You are declared righteous by God;[51]
8) You enter a love relationship with God;[52] and
9) God accepts you.[53]

Jesus is a Saviour worth having and the Christian life is worth living.

You, too, can come to Jesus, just as you are, wherever you are. God's grace is still available for all today. Let the hymn "Just as I am" be your song of confidence.

Just as I am

1. Just as I am, without one plea,
   But that Thy blood was shed for me,
   And that Thou bids't me come to Thee
   O Lamb of God, I come! I come!

2. Just as I am, and waiting not
   To rid my soul of one dark blot;
   To Thee whose blood can cleanse each spot,
   O Lamb of God, I come, I come!

3. Just as I am, though tossed about
   With many a conflict, many a doubt;
   Fightings within, and fears without,
   O Lamb of God, I come, I come!

4. Just as I am, poor, wretched, blind;
   Sight, riches, healing of the mind;
   Yes, all I need, in Thee to find,
   O Lamb of God, I come, I come!

5. Just as I am, Thou wilt receive,
   Wilt welcome, pardon, cleanse, relieve;
   Because Thy promise I believe,
   O Lamb of God, I come, I come!

6. Just as I am, Thy love unknown
   Has broken every barrier down;
   Now, to be Thine, yea, Thine alone
   O Lamb of God, I come, I come!

Charlotte Elliott (1789-1871)

CHAPTER THREE

THE FISH GATE

"And He (Jesus) said unto them, go ye into all the world, and preach the gospel to every creature."[54]

-MARK 16:15, KJV

T he Fish Gate was so named because the fishermen of Galilee would bring their fish in through this gate to be sold. It was in the northern wall next to the tower of Hananeel. This tower was part of the city's defence system and was situated near the citadel, where the soldiers guarded the temple and protected the northern approach to the city, which was especially vulnerable. The Fish Gate reminds us of the time when Jesus called his first disciples.

"And Jesus, walking by the sea of Galilee, saw two brethren, Simon called Peter, and Andrew his brother, casting a net into the sea: for they were fishers. And he said to them, follow me, and I will make you fishers of men. And they straightway left their nets and followed him."[55]

-MATTHEW 4:18–20, KJV

Fishing is a symbol of witnessing to others. We tell others that we belong to Christ. We witness by our words and actions, and it is a natural progression in our Christian life that after receiving Jesus as our Lord and Saviour we would then want to tell others about it. It was a major objective of the ministry of Jesus. He told them:

"The harvest is plentiful, but the workers are few. Ask the Lord of the harvest, therefore, to send out workers into his harvest field. Go! I am sending you out like lambs among wolves."[56]

-LUKE 10:2–4, NIV

Jesus' last direct command before He ascended to heaven was:

Therefore go and make disciples of all nations, baptizing them in the name of the Father and of the Son and the Holy Spirit, and teaching them to obey everything I have commanded you."[57]

-MATHEW 28:19–20, KJV

Jesus speaking to Peter:

"The third time he said to him, 'Simon son of John, do you love me?' Peter was hurt because Jesus asked him the third time, 'Do you love me?' He said, 'Lord, you know all things; you know that I love you.' Jesus said, 'feed my sheep.'"[58]

-JOHN 21:17–18, KJV

In fact, this is known as the 'Great Commission'!
And again, after the resurrection:

"And Jesus came and spake unto them, saying, all power is given unto me in heaven and earth. Go ye therefore, and teach all nations, baptizing them in the name of the Father, and of the Son, and of the Holy Spirit: Teaching them to observe all things whatsoever I have commanded you: and, lo, I am with you always, even unto the end of the world"[59] *(Mathew 28:18–20, KJV).*

Paul asked the Thessalonians, "For what is our hope or joy, or crown of rejoicing? Are not even ye in the presence of our Lord Jesus Christ at his coming? For you are our glory and joy."[60] The crown of rejoicing is the soul-winner's crown. The most significant work we are privileged to do for the Lord is to bring others to the knowledge of Christ as personal Saviour.

We are reminded that: a) it is wise to win souls to Christ,[61] b) it is a work against sin to win souls to Christ,[62] c) it is a cause for joy in heaven to win souls to Christ,[63] and d) every soul winner will shine as the stars forever.[64] We must witness, therefore, with our lives so that others may see Christ in us,[65] and with our mouths, trusting the Holy Spirit to give power to the spoken word,[66] remembering that our labour is not in vain in the Lord.[67]

It is the soul-winner alone who will receive the **crown of rejoicing**, with all of heaven rejoicing with him. Once we have come to know our Lord and Saviour, we are commanded to tell others about it. We must obey the Great Commission or condemn the people we love and care about, the people Jesus died for, to a lost eternity. In 1966, at an Inter-School Christian Fellowship youth camp at Victory Heights in Trinidad and Tobago, I wrote this song, "**I Am a Debtor**," assisted by my counsellor, Dennis Minott

I am a debtor obligated, to the people of the world.
I must tell them, tell them of my Lord. (Repeat)
Are you one of His?
Have you told them of this?
You must; you must, you must.
I am a debtor, obligated, to the people of the world.
I must tell them, tell them of my Lord

Yes, after receiving Jesus as our Lord and Saviour, we are commanded to pass through the Fish Gate, to become "fishers of men," to spread the good news of Jesus Christ to others.

We must tell the people in this world that Jesus saves! Jesus saves! In 1898, Priscilla Jane Owens wrote the beautiful hymn "**We have Heard the Joyful Song**" that is still relevant for us today.

We Have Heard the Joyful Song

1. *We have heard the joyful sound:*
   Jesus saves! Jesus saves!
   Spread the gladness all around:
   Jesus saves! Jesus saves!
   Bear the news to every land,
   Climb the steeps and cross the waves;
   Onward! 'tis our Lord's command:
   Jesus saves! Jesus saves!

2. *Sing above the battle strife:*
   Jesus saves! Jesus saves!
   By His death and endless life,
   Jesus saves! Jesus saves!
   Sing it softly through the gloom,
   When the heart for mercy craves;
   Sing in triumph o'er the tomb:
   Jesus saves! Jesus saves!

3. *Give the winds a mighty voice:*
   Jesus saves! Jesus saves!
   Let the nations now rejoice:
   Jesus saves! Jesus saves!
   Shout salvation full and free;
   Highest hills and deepest caves;
   This our song of victory:
   Jesus saves, Jesus saves!

Priscilla Jane Owens (1829- 1907)

CHAPTER FOUR

THE OLD GATE

"But as He who called you is holy, you also be holy in all your conduct, because it is written, "Be holy, for I am holy."" [68]

-*1 PETER 1:15, KJV*

'Pursue peace with all people, and holiness, without which no one will see the Lord." [69]

-*HEBREWS 12:14, KJV*

The Old Gate[70] or the "Jeshanah" gate was the corner gate[71] located at the north-west corner of the city. It was identified with the "Mishneh Gate." The Hebrew word means "New Quarter." In Nehemiah's day, the north-west section of the city was called the Mishneh or New Quarter, and this gate led into it. It was repaired by the Jebusites. It is said:

"Moreover the old gate repaired Jehoiada the son of Paseah, and Meshullam the son of Besodeiah; they laid the beams thereof and set up the doors thereof, and the locks thereof, and the bars thereof." [72]

25

During the dedication ceremony of the wall around Jerusalem the gate is listed among the gates the choir procession passed over as they circled the city in celebration.[73]

After experiencing the Sheep Gate and becoming a Christian, and then sharing our faith with others, thus passing through the Fish Gate, we must now walk the talk. When we turn aside to enter through the Old Gate, we remember Moses:

> *"So when the LORD saw that he turned aside to look, God called to him from the midst of the bush and said, '****Moses, Moses!****' And he said, 'Here I am.' Then He said, 'Do not draw near this place. Take your sandals off your feet, ****for the place where you stand is holy ground.**** I am the God of your father – the God of Abraham, the God of Isaac, and the God of Jacob. Come now, therefore, and I will send you to Pharaoh that you may bring My people, the children of Israel, out of Egypt.'"*[74]
>
> *-EXODUS 3:4, 6A; 10, KJV*

The Old Gate reminds us that holiness is not optional. The holiness of God is His standard for mankind and He places a responsibility on us as his children to live up to His standard. It was the time when we were introduced to the holiness of God and the legacy of our fathers in the faith. It was at this "gate" that I heard the call from God to serve Him in ministry and I answered, "Here I am." You are admonished, "as obedient children, do not conform to the evil desires you had when you lived in ignorance; but just as He who called you is holy, so be holy in all you do; for it is written: 'Be holy because I am holy.'"[75] Moses declared: "Speak to all the congregation of the children of Israel and say to them: 'You shall be holy, for I the LORD your God *am* holy.'"[76] "And you shall be holy to Me, for I the LORD *am* holy, and have separated you from the peoples, that you should be Mine."[77]

The writer of Hebrews declared: "Follow peace with all men, and **holiness, without** which **no man** shall see the Lord."[78] We must, therefore, consecrate our lives to God and live a holy life. The Hebrew word for "holy" means *"to be morally clean*; to be consecrated, dedicated, hallowed; to be free from sin, to purify, to sanctify." Therefore, to be holy is to be morally blameless; it is to be separated from sin and thus to be consecrated to God, to be set apart unto God. The word signifies separation unto God and conducting ourselves befitting of those so separated.

An overview of the New Testament reveals how the writers defined holiness. Paul contrasted a life of holiness with a life of immorality and impurity. He proclaimed:

> *"For this is the will of God even your sanctification,* (separated and set apart for pure and holy living)*: that ye should abstain from fornication* (the root word for fornication is 'fornoia,' which means all forms of sexual vices and perversions)*; that every one of you should know how to possess* (control, manage) *his vessel in sanctification* (purity separated from things profane) *and honour, not [to be used] in the lust of concupiscence, even as the gentiles which know not God."*[79]

Holiness requires us to live a life of obedience to God, not conforming to the evil desires that governed us in our former ignorance, when we did not know the requirements of the gospel. Peter reminds us that we are a chosen generation, a royal priesthood, a holy nation, a peculiar people; that we should shew forth the praises of him who hath called us out of darkness into his marvellous light.[80] John contrasted one who is holy with those who do wrong and are vile. He said, "And he who is righteous (just, upright, in right standing with God), let him be righteous still; and he who is holy, let him be holy still."[81]

We must apply what Paul told us when he said:

"I beseech you, therefore, brethren, by the mercies of God, that ye present your bodies a living sacrifice, holy, acceptable unto God, which is your reasonable service. And be not conformed to this world: but be ye transformed by the renewing of your mind, that ye may prove what is that good, and acceptable, and perfect, will of God. "[82]

-ROMANS 12:1–2, KJV

Paul again affirmed:

"For this is the will of God, your sanctification: that you should abstain from sexual immorality; that each of you should know how to possess his vessel in sanctification and honour, not in passion of lust, like the Gentiles who do not know God; that no one should take advantage of and defraud his brother in this matter, because the Lord *is* the avenger of all such, as we also forewarned you and testified. For God did not call us to uncleanness, but to holiness. Therefore, he who rejects *this* does not reject man, but God, who has also given us His Holy Spirit."[83] In the book of Deuteronomy, Israel was admonished to: "Remember the days of old; consider the long generations past." When people refused to do so, God turned against them. The prophet Jeremiah commanded them to: "Stand at the crossroads and look; ask for the ancient paths, ask where the good way is, and walk in it, and you will find rest for your souls."[84] And when "His people remembered the days of old, the days of Moses and his people,"[85] they remembered how God's hand was mighty and powerful to save. They turned back to Him, and He saved them.

Remember Joseph. He was the eleventh son of Jacob and the first son and child of Jacob's beloved Rachael.[86] The record of his life presents him as being flawless. He was undoubtedly among the most outstanding characters of the Bible. The account of his marvellous life covers almost fourteen full chapters. In a number of chapters or narrative concentration, the recorded history of Joseph is much longer than that of Isaac's and Jacob's, or even of Abraham's.

The Bible confirms that Joseph was outstanding in spiritual superiority. The beauty of Joseph's superior spiritual standing is seen in the righteousness of his principles. He could not disappoint his master (Potiphar), who trusted him.[87] He could not defile another's wife, even though she tempted him. To have done so would have been in God's sight and his "great wickedness."[88] He could not dishonour his God, who transformed and taught him. He understood, long before the divine insight given to David, that to sin against his God-created neighbour is to sin against his God.[89]

Joseph came through not one temptation and refusal situation but many, all with distinction. He was tempted by a passionate, polluted woman day after day, but he stood his ground. Genesis 39:8–10 declares his stand. He did not lie with her. He did not act light with her. He did not look at her. He did not even listen to her. Far from "going all the way," he did not go even part of the way. In fact, he went the other way.

When temptations come, remember that "No **temptation** has overtaken you except what is common to mankind. And God *is* faithful; and He will not let you be tempted beyond what you can bear. **But** when you are tempted, He will also provide a way out so that you can endure it."[90] When trials come, enter through the Old Gate to learn the ways of truth that never change. When your faith is tested, when circumstances crowd around you that seem too big to overcome, when it seems that the problems are even too big for God, enter through the "Old Gate." Get into God's Word.

Remember when you first accepted Jesus as your Lord and Saviour at the Fish Gate. Never forget the joy of your salvation, nor lose your love for God. At the Old Gate God wants us to make a total surrender of our lives to Him. He wants all of us. He wants our time, talents, thoughts, finances, hopes, aspirations, reputation, hobbies, friendships, habits and future. God wants to be the Lord and master of every single part of our lives. He knows what is best for us. He wants to direct, guide, use and change us into the image of His Son, Jesus Christ.

In the Beatitudes, Jesus said, "Blessed are the pure in heart: for they shall see God."[91] The fact is that "God is light, and in him is no darkness at all." Therefore, if we are to see God, we must know the light of holiness in our lives. Jesus said, "I am the light of the world. Whoever follows me will never walk in darkness."[92] Remember, "the path of the just is as the shining light, that shineth more and more unto the perfect day."[93] Finally, at the Old Gate, we must always remember *Jehovah-M'Kaddesh,* which means Jehovah who sanctifies, and his command: "Sanctify yourselves therefore and be ye holy: for I am Jehovah your God... I am Jehovah which sanctify you" (Leviticus 20:7, 8, KJV). The full tribute voiced to Jehovah is in words: "Who is like unto thee, O Jehovah ... glorious in holiness" (Exodus 15: 11, KJV). The cry of the Seraphim, who veil their eyes in the presence of God's holiness, is "Holy, holy, holy, is the Lord of hosts": and then, "the whole earth is full of his glory" (Isaiah 6:3, KJV).

It is against the glory of God's holiness that all have sinned, for this is what the apostle Paul meant when he said: "All have sinned and come short of the glory of God" (Romans 3:23, KJV). It is the glory and beauty of His holiness that God wishes to impart to us. The prayer of the psalmist speaks volumes when he says: "Let the beauty of Jehovah our God be upon us" (Psalm 90:17a, KJV).

What Jehovah was to His people in the Old Testament, the Lord Jesus Christ is to us in the New Testament. He was altogether holy and spotless in His life and was "in all points tempted like as we are, yet without sin" (Hebrews 4:15, KJV). He became our High Priest "who is holy, harmless, undefiled, separate from sinners, and made higher than the heavens" (Hebrews 7:26, KJV). He was made sin for us, in His redeeming love, but He Himself knew no sin (II Corinthians 5:21, KJV). We are commanded to present our bodies as a living sacrifice, holy, and acceptable unto God, (Romans. 12:1, KJV). Our new man is created in righteousness and true holiness (Eph. 4:24, KJV). We are Christ's workmanship created in Him unto good works in which we are to walk (Ephesians. 2:10, KJV), and which we are to maintain (Titus 3:8, KJV).

God wants us to share in His character and works and to be separate and apart from all evil and wickedness. This desire is not to be negative but to be good. Holiness is positive and active. We must be holy in practice. God has endowed us with free will. He commands His people to be holy, but He will not force them to be so. We must of our own free will exercise that provision and power.

To all the youths who are reading the pages of this book: flee youthful lusts; resist the devil, and he will flee from you; shun the very appearance of evil; grieve not the Holy Spirit of God and as William Dunn Longstaff, 1882, wrote, take time to be holy. Your conduct matters to God.

Take Time to Be Holy

1. *Take time to be holy, speak oft with thy Lord;*
   Abide in Him always, and feed on His Word.
   Make friends of God's children; help those who are weak,
   Forgetting in nothing, His blessing to seek.

2. *Take time to be holy; the world rushes on;*
   Spend much time in secret, with Jesus alone.
   By looking to Jesus, like Him thou shalt be;
   Thy friends in thy conduct. His likeness shall see.

3. *Take time to be holy, let Him be thy Guide;*
   And run not before Him, whatever betide.
   In joy or sorrow, still, follow the Lord,
   And, looking to Jesus, still, trust in His Word.

4. *Take time to be holy, be calm in thy soul,*
   Each thought and each motive under His control.
   Thus led by His Spirit to fountains of love,
   Thou soon shalt be fitted for service above.

In 1900, Lelia N. Morris wrote this beautiful hymn for us, "**Called Unto Holiness**," which has been an anthem for the Holiness Movement for over 100 years. Let this hymn be your song of praise.

Called Unto Holiness

1. "Called unto holiness," church of our God,
   Purchase of Jesus, redeemed by His blood;
   Called from the world and its idols to flee,
   Called from the bondage of sin to be free.

2. Refrain:
   "Holiness unto the Lord" is our watchword and song,
   "Holiness unto the Lord" as we're marching along;
   Sing it, shout it, loud and long,
   "Holiness unto the Lord," now and forever.

3. "Called unto holiness," children of light,
   Walking with Jesus in garments of white;
   Raiment unsullied, nor tarnished with sin;
   God's Holy Spirit is abiding within.

4. "Called unto holiness," praise His dear Name!
   This blessed secret to faith now made plain:
   Not our righteousness, but Christ within,
   Living, and reigning, and saving from sin.

5. "Called unto holiness," bride of the Lamb,
   Waiting the Bridegroom's returning!
   Lift up your heads, for the day draweth near
   When in His beauty the King shall appear.

CHAPTER FIVE

THE VALLEY GATE

"...count it all joy when ye fall into divers temptations; Knowing this, that the trying of your faith worketh patience. But let patience have her perfect work, that ye may be perfect and entire, wanting nothing.[94] *Blessed is the man that endureth temptation; for when he is tried, he shall receive the crown of life, which the Lord hath promised to them that love him.*"[95]

-JAMES 1:2–4, 12, KJV

The Valley Gate[96] was located at the south-western corner of Jerusalem. Several valleys surrounded Jerusalem, and this gate opened out to the valley of Hinnom. We can learn much from the lengthy sections of walls between the Valley Gate and the Old Gate. The Valley Gate and its adjacent walls required lots of repairs and had to be done by the largest teams on the project. This gate speaks of humility, sufferings, and testing. It is in the valleys that we see vegetation. Our spiritual growth occurs when we are walking through the "valleys," the trials and tribulations that come our way.

The following Scriptures speak to us about how we are to respond in the valley:

▶ None of you should turn back because of these persecutions. You yourselves know that such persecutions are part of God's will for us.[97]

▶ "We all have to experience many hardships," they said, "before we enter the kingdom of God."[98]

▶ Moses said to the people, "Do not be afraid. God has come to test you so that the fear of God will be with you to keep you from sinning."[99]

▶ Praise our God, O peoples, let the sound of his praise be heard; he has preserved our lives and kept our feet from slipping. For you, O God tested us; you refined us like silver. You brought us into prison and laid burdens on our backs. You let people ride over our heads; we went through fire and water, but you brought us to a place of abundance.[100]

▶ For Christ suffered for you and left you a personal example so that you might follow in his footsteps. He was guilty of no sin... When he was insulted, he offered no insult in return. When he suffered, he made no threats of revenge. He merely committed his cause to the One who judges justly.[101]

▶ Yea and all that will live godly in Christ Jesus shall suffer persecution.[102]

▶ Wherein ye greatly rejoice, though now for a season, if need be, ye are in heaviness through manifold temptations: That the trial of your faith, being much more precious than of gold that Perisheth, though it be tried with fire, might be found unto praise and honour and glory at the appearing of Jesus Christ.[103]

▶ Beloved, think it not strange concerning the fiery trial which is to try you, as though some strange thing happened unto you: But rejoice, inasmuch as ye are partakers of Christ's sufferings; that, when his glory shall be revealed, ye may be glad also with exceeding joy. If ye be reproached for the name of Christ, happy are ye; for the spirit of glory and of God resteth upon you: on their part, he is evil spoken of, but on your part, he is glorified.[104]

- ▸ And not only so, but we glory in tribulations also: knowing that tribulation worketh patience, and patience, experience; and experience, hope: And hope maketh not ashamed; because the love of God is shed abroad in our hearts by the Holy Ghost which is given unto us.[105]

- ▸ Blessed be God, even the Father of our Lord Jesus Christ, the Father of mercies, and the God of all comfort; Who comforteth us in all our tribulation, that we may be able to comfort them which are in any trouble, by the comfort wherewith we ourselves are comforted of God. For as the sufferings of Christ abound in us, so our consolation also aboundeth by Christ.[106]

- ▸ Blessed is the man that endureth **temptation:** for when he is tried, he shall receive the crown of life, which the Lord hath promised to them that love him.[107]

In the Psalms, we read about the victory in the valley. Here is what it says:

> *"Yea, though I walk through the valley of the shadow of death, I will fear no evil: for thou art with me; thy rod and thy staff they comfort me. Thou preparest a table before me in the presence of mine enemies: thou anointest my head with oil; my cup runneth over. Surely goodness and mercy shall follow me all the days of my life: and I will dwell in the house of the Lord forever."*[108]

In the valley, remember the experiences of the prophet Ezekiel,[109] for it was in a valley with many dry and very dry bones scattered on the ground, the skeletons of corpses long ago decomposed, that he had a vision from the LORD Jehovah of the many people who were slain.[110] These bodies were left on the battlefield to become food for the vultures to eat and objects for the sun to bleach. It was in the valley where the Lord told Ezekiel to walk around among the bones, so he could appreciate their vast number and see how dry they were.

In the valley, the Lord asked him, "Can these bones live?" In the valley, God told him to prophesy to the dry and very dry bones, and Ezekiel spoke to them, and they came together. Then, their skeletons were covered with flesh and skin so that what was lying there in the valley looked like a sleeping army. The bodies lacked only one thing: **life**. And God commanded Ezekiel to prophesy to the wind and told him to speak to the bones. When Ezekiel spoke the living Word of God, the breath of God entered the dead bodies, and they lived and stood to their feet.

In the valley, the Lord explained the meaning of the vision. Ezekiel learned that nothing is impossible with God and that it is God who quickeneth the dead, and calleth those things which be not as though they were."[111] The vision reminds us that the Word of the Lord is "alive and active."[112] It not only *has* life, but it *imparts* life.[113] Jesus said, "The words that I speak unto you, they are spirit, and they are life."[114]

Paul told us that until the Holy Spirit quickens men and women to the spiritual life, they are "...dead in trespasses and sins."[115] This can be true of you, your spouse, your parents or your children: *though full of life physically, you can be dead spiritually. You may believe that you are* spiritually useless, for unbleached bones may have a purpose, but when 'very dry' they are worthless; it only remains for them to be gathered and burned. Paul declared, *"They have together become unprofitable."*[116] *You may also believe that you are* spiritually hopeless, but God said to speak to the dry bones and say, "Oh! Dry bones, hear the word of the LORD." There is power in the Word of God.

It is only the Word of God that can effect such miracles, for it is living and powerful, and sharper than any two-edged sword, piercing even to the division of soul and spirit, and joints and marrow, and is a discerner of the thoughts and intents of the heart.[117]

In Isaiah, we read: *"So shall My word be that goes forth from My mouth; it shall not return to Me void, but it shall accomplish what I please, and it shall prosper in the thing for which I sent it"*[118] (Isaiah 55:11, KJV). In the valley, you can have life, hope and be empowered by the Holy Spirit.

When you are in the valley, you must also remember the garden at Gethsemane. It is located on the slope of the Mount of Olives just across the Kidron Valley from Jerusalem. It was the place where Jesus prayed most, was forsaken, betrayed with a kiss and experienced great sufferings. It was at Gethsemane, when Jesus wanted companionship as He faced the cross, and He selected Peter, James and John, the same men who had accompanied Him to the home of Jairus[119] and to the Mount of Transfiguration[120] to watch with Him in the Garden of Gethsemane. These three experiences are parallel: "That I may know Him[121] [Mount of Transfiguration], and the power of His resurrection [home of Jairus], and the fellowship in His sufferings [garden of Gethsemane].

Jesus' struggle in the garden can be understood only in the light of what would happen to Him on the cross: He would be made sin for us[122] and bear the curse of the law.[123] It was not the physical suffering that almost overwhelmed Him with "anguish and sorrow," but the contemplation of being forsaken by His Father.[124] This was "the cup" that He would drink.[125]

At Gethsemane, He called for Abba, an Aramaic word that means "papa" or "daddy." There was no response. He was forsaken. There, Jesus revealed to us again the intimate relationship He had with His Father. Note that Jesus did not tell the Father what to do. He had perfect confidence in His will. Three times He prayed about the matter, and each time He yielded to the Father's will in loving surrender. It was at Gethsemane He admonished his disciples, who were sleeping while he was praying, to "watch and pray," an admonition that is often repeated in Scripture.[126]

It was in the garden, after He was arrested, that all His disciples left him, fled and were scattered. Jesus was left alone with His enemies, and yet He was not alone, because the Father was with Him.[127] You can learn from Jesus, should your prayer garden of **Gethsemane** be turned into a garden of suffering, betrayal, agony and you are abandoned and burdened. I can identify with this quotation by one of our great gospel singers:

"It is in the quiet crucible of your personal, private sufferings that your noblest dreams are born, and God's greatest gifts are given in compensation for what you have been through."

– Wintley Phipps

When digging in the valley, Isaac's servants found a well of springing water.[128]The purpose of digging was to find water and, spiritually, we are to dig deeper than the outer surface to find what God has in store for us.

Ezekiel said, "For the Lord your God is bringing you into a good land, a land of brooks of water, of fountains and springs, that flow out of valleys and hills."[129] The journey of the Christian through the valley is never easy, but *Jehovah-rohi* (which means **Jehovah, my Shepherd) is always with you.** *Jehovah-rohi* begins the twenty-third psalm, where it is translated, "The Lord is my shepherd." Commit the twenty-third psalm to memory. It will comfort your life in closing years. It will dry many tears and dispel many fears through-out your life. You will look back upon the stormy, troubled seasons of your life in the valley when you were hunted by the enemy of your soul; then through the years of warfare and at times sorrow; and you will find God's goodness and guiding presence through it all.

Jehovah -rohi is your Keeper. He will not allow the sun to smite you by day nor the moon by night. He shall keep you from all evil. He neither slumbers nor sleeps (Psalm 121, KJV). The prophet Isaiah says of Him: "Behold the Lord God will come with strong hand . He shall feed his flock like a shepherd. He shall gently lead (Isaiah 40: 10-11, NKJV). Our shepherd is both strong and gentle.

Jehovah-rohi is your Shepherd. You can say: "You know when I sit and when I rise; you perceive my thoughts from afar. You discern my going out and my lying down; you are familiar with all my ways" (Psalm 139:2-3, NIV). Indeed, you can have personal experiences with a personal God to whom every sheep of the fold is precious. You can have His particular care.

In the New Testament, the name *Jehovah-rohi* is that glorious Shepherd of the sheep. He is our Lord Jesus Christ. He goes after the sheep that was lost. He says:

"I am the good shepherd: the good shepherd giveth his life for the sheep. I am the good shepherd, and know my sheep, and am known of mine. As the Father knoweth me, even so, know I the Father: and I lay down my life for the sheep"

-JOHN 10: 11,14-15, KJV

He is also the "great shepherd of the sheep" (Hebrews 13:20, KJV). He is touched with the feeling of our infirmities, for He was tempted and tried in all points as we are, yet without sin (Hebrews 4:15, KJV). He Himself learned obedience and was made perfect through sufferings (Hebrews 2:10, KJV). For as a lamb, He subjected Himself willingly to the Father's will, when "it pleased Jehovah to bruise him" and to "make his soul an offering for sin" (Isaiah 53: 10, KJV), so that while all we like sheep had gone astray, Jehovah laid on Him the iniquity of us all. He was led as a lamb to the slaughter (Isaiah 53:6, 7, KJV) and He bore our sins.

As the good and great Shepherd of the sheep, He meets every need of His flock (Philippians 4:19, KJV), and there is no want to those who trust him. He leads us into the green pastures of His Word and feeds us upon the true Bread of Life. He guides us into right paths, and we are assured of His continuous presence.

The Holy Spirit of truth, He promised, will guide you into all truth (John 16:13, KJV). "I will pray to the Father," He said, "and he shall give you another Comforter, that he may abide with you forever" (John 14:16, KJV). For the Shepherd and the sheep are never separated. By day He gently leads, and by night He is the door of the sheep (John 10:9, 10, KJV). He protects us from the perils that torment us, and our perils are very real. We are safe in the protection of His table spread before us even in the presence of the enemies. He knows every one of us by name. He knows the particular need of each one of us. He knows our peculiarities. He knows our weaknesses.

When we are severely tried, He will lead gently on. When we are weary or wounded, He will anoint our heads, heal our wounds and refresh us with tender care. We are led away by some at times. Sometimes the path is through fresh green meadows; sometimes over rough, steep, rocky paths, perhaps through dark places where the sun scarcely shines. After the heat and burden of the day, He gathers us into the fold, where there is no more fear but comfort and safety. And then we know that whatever the sufferings and sorrows, the trials and terrors of the day, His goodness and loving-kindness will follow us all the days of our lives. In the valley, we must go all the way with Jesus as expressed in the great hymn below written by William O. Cushing in 1878.

Down in the Valley with My Saviour I would Go

1. Down in the valley with my Saviour, I would go,
   Where the flowers are blooming, and the sweet waters flow;
   Everywhere He leads me I will follow, follow on,
   Walking in His footsteps until the crown is won.

   Chorus:
   Follow! Follow! I will follow Jesus!
   Anywhere, everywhere, I will follow on!
   Follow! Follow! I will follow Jesus!
   Everywhere He leads me I will follow on!

2. Down in the valley with my Saviour, I would go,
   Where the storms are sweeping, and the dark waters flow;
   With His hand to lead me, I will never, never fear,
   Danger cannot fright me if my Lord is near. (Chorus)

3. Down in the valley or upon the mountain steep,
   Close beside my Saviour would my soul ever keep;
   He will lead me safely on the path that He has trod,
   Up to where they gather on the hills of God.

William O. Cushing (1801-1900).

CHAPTER SIX

THE DUNG GATE

"That you put off, concerning your former conduct, the old man which grows corrupt according to the deceitful lusts, and be renewed in the spirit of your mind, and that you put on the new man which was created according to God, in true righteousness and holiness."[130]

-EPHESIANS 4:22–24, NKJV

The Dung Gate [131]was located at the southernmost point of the city, near the pool of Siloam. It was the main exit to the valley of Hinnom, where the city disposed of its garbage. It was perhaps called as such because more refuse was carried out *through this gate* to the general dump heap than was done through any other. The first mention of dung is about sacrifices. The law required that the dung and certain parts of the animal not be burned on the altar, but outside the camp.[132] Dung was used as fuel.[133] During the summer, in some villages, it was gathered and mixed with straw, made into cakes and dried, and used for heat in the winter or for cooking all through the year when there was no wood or other fuel. It burned slowly like peat and met the needs in various places.

While the Valley Gate teaches us how to walk through testing and trials and their importance, the Dung Gate speaks of the works of the flesh. Through the Dung Gate, refuse was taken out of Jerusalem, to the valley of Hinnom, where it was burnt.

In the same way that trash would not have been left to stink up the city, so must sin be taken out of the heart of the believer and destroyed. There are some things we must put off.

In Proverbs, we are admonished to put off perversity.[134] James admonished us to get rid of rebellion and evil-speaking, envying and strife, or there would be confusion and evil work.[135] In his letter to the Ephesians, Paul taught us to:

- ▶ put away lying,
- ▶ refuse to give place to the devil,
- ▶ put away stealing
- ▶ not corrupt the communication that comes out of your mouth,
- ▶ not grieve the Holy Spirit of God, and
- ▶ let all bitterness, wrath, anger, clamour and evil-speaking be put away from you, with all malice.[136]

Paul instructed us to walk in the Spirit so that we would not fulfil the lust of the flesh and therefore put off the works of the flesh. These are: adultery, fornication, uncleanness, hatred, lasciviousness, idolatry, witchcraft, variance, emulations, wrath, strife, seditions, heresies, envyings, murders, drunkenness, reveling and such like. He affirmed that those who do such things shall not inherit the kingdom of God.[137]

Paul also taught us in Romans to put off all unrighteousness, fornication, wickedness, covetousness, maliciousness; envy, murder, debate, deceit, malignancy; gossiping, backbiting, hate for God, being spiteful, pride, boasting, inventing evil things, disobedience to parents, lack of understanding, covenant breaking, lack of natural affection, cruelty and, cold-heartedness. Paul declared that God's judgment is that they who commit such things are worthy of death, especially those who not only do them but have pleasure in doing so.[138]

The Dung Gate, therefore, urges us to "walk worthily of the calling wherewith we were called, with all lowliness and meekness"[139] and "…that we must no longer walk in the vanity of our minds… but we must be renewed in the spirit of our minds."[140] We are also commanded to walk in love, even as Christ also loved us and gave himself for us.[141] Paul also admonished us to "walk as children of light… Proving what is well-pleasing unto the Lord"[142] (Ephesians 5:8, 10, KJV). The writer of the Hebrews reminded us that:

> "…we also, since we are surrounded by so great a cloud of witnesses, let us lay aside every weight, and the sin which so easily ensnares us, and let us run with endurance the race that is set before us, looking unto Jesus, the author and finisher of our faith, who for the joy that was set before Him endured the cross, despising the shame, and has sat down at the right hand of the throne of God."[143]
>
> *-HEBREWS 12:12, KJV*

The apostle Paul told Timothy: *"be strong in the grace that is in Christ Jesus and endure hardness, as a good soldier of Jesus Christ.* No one engaged in warfare entangles himself with the affairs of this life that he may please him who enlisted him as a soldier. Be diligent to present yourself approved to God, a worker who does not need to be ashamed, rightly dividing the word of truth. But shun profane and idle babblings, for they will increase to more ungodliness. ***If a man, therefore, purges himself from these***, *he shall be a vessel unto honour, sanctified, and meet for the master's use, and prepared unto every good work. Flee also youthful lusts: but follow righteousness, faith, charity, peace, with them that call on the Lord out of a pure heart."-[144]-* An incorruptible crown will be given to those who master the old nature (1 Corinthians 9:25-27, KJV). So at the Dung Gate, we must pray and ask God to search our hearts, get rid of the "dung" and set us free.

Search Me, O God

1. *Search me, O God, and know my heart today,*
   Try me, O Saviour, know my thoughts, I pray;
   See if there be some wicked way in me;
   Cleanse me from every sin, and set me free.

2. *I praise Thee, Lord, for cleansing me from sin;*
   Fulfil Thy word and make me pure within;
   Fill me with fire, where once I burned with shame;
   Grant my desire to magnify Thy name.

3. *Lord, take my life, and make it wholly Thine;*
   Fill my poor heart with Thy great love divine;
   Take all my will, my passion, self, and pride;
   I now surrender, Lord, in me abide.

4. *O Holy Spirit, revival comes from Thee;*
   Send a revival, start the work in me;
   Thy Word declares Thou will supply our need;
   For blessings now, O Lord, I humbly plead.

James Edwin Orr (1912-1987)

CHAPTER SEVEN

THE FOUNTAIN GATE

"And do not be drunk with wine, in which is dissipation; but be filled with the Holy Spirit, speaking to one another in psalms and hymns and spiritual songs, singing and making melody in your heart to the Lord."[145]

-EPHESIANS 5:18–19, KJV

A fountain is a natural source of flowing water from underground. Fountains always empty themselves into low places; they flow in the valleys of the earth. The Fountain Gate[146] was on the eastern wall, just north of the Dung Gate, in a strategic location near the pool of Siloam,[147] where water flowed. It is called the water of Shiloah.[148] It was not until the time of King Hezekiah that the first tunnel aqueduct, Siloam's most famous work, was made.[149] The Fountain Gate was located close to the Dung Gate.

At the time of Nehemiah and afterwards, many washed before they entered the temple area. The pool of Siloam was also the place where Jesus sent the blind man to wash.[150] Jesus said, "Whoever believes in me, as the Scripture has said, streams of living water will flow from within him."[151] The Holy Spirit is symbolized here as streams of flowing water, like a fountain. The **Fountain Gate**, therefore, speaks of the Holy Spirit.

I want you to know and always remember that the Holy Spirit of God is a **person**. He has a mind.[152] He searches the human mind.[153] He has a will.[154] He forbids.[155] He permits.[156] He speaks.

He spoke to Phillip in a desert;[157] Peter on a housetop;[158] some elders in Antioch;[159] and to the seven churches in Asia Minor[160] on no less than seven occasions.[161] He loves.[162] He grieves.[163] He prays and offers up fervent and effectual prayers for you.[164] He is omnipresent; you cannot hide from Him. He is omniscient.[165] He searches all things, even the more profound things of God; you need Him. He is omnipotent; you need His wisdom and guidance.

Remember, your body is the temple of the Holy Spirit,[166] and as a Christian, you are the temple of the living God.[167] He is called the Spirit of God,[168] of Christ,[169] of truth,[170] of grace,[171] of glory,[172] of life,[173] of wisdom and revelation,[174] of promise,[175] of adoption,[176] of holiness,[177] and of faith,[178] and He is the Comforter.[179] I tell you, without Him, you can do nothing.

> Jesus assured us that *"when He, the Spirit of truth, has come, He will guide you into all truth; for He will not speak on His authority, but whatever He hears He will speak; and He will tell you things to come. He will glorify Me, for He will take of what is Mine and declare it to you. All things that the Father has are Mine. Therefore, I said that He would take of Mine and declare it to you."*[180]
>
> *-JOHN 16:13–15, KJV*

We must go to the Fountain Gate and allow the Holy Spirit to empower us for a living, for "…this is the word of the Lord unto Zerubbabel, saying, not by might, nor by power, but by my Spirit, says the Lord of hosts."[181]

Jesus declared, *"But you shall receive power, after that the Holy Spirit comes upon you: and ye shall be witnesses unto me both in Jerusalem, and in all Judaea, and in Samaria, and unto the uttermost part of the earth."*[182]

The following is a summary of the work that the Holy Spirit does in our lives:

1. He regenerates the believing sinner, i.e., recreates him and gives him the nature of God.[183]
2. He baptises us.[184]
3. He indwells the believer.[185]
4. He seals the believer.[186]
5. He fills the believer.[187]
6. He blesses believers by:
    - praying for them,[188]
    - guiding them,[189]
    - teaching them,[190]
    - empowering them for witnessing,[191]
    - imparting the love of God in them and through them,[192]
    - conforming them to the image of Christ,[193]
    - strengthening their new nature,[194]
    - revealing biblical truths to them,[195]
    - leading them into all truths,[196]
    - recalling and clarifying the works of Jesus to them[197] and helping them to understand the Scriptures,
    - assuring them concerning salvation and services,[198]
    - giving them liberty,[199]
    - filling their mouths with words to speak,[200]
    - interceding for them[201] so that the Lord's will be done, and
    - bestowing extraordinary gifts upon them within the body of Christ.[202]

Paul declared, "This I say then, walk in the Spirit, and ye shall not fulfil the lust of the flesh. For the flesh lusts against the Spirit, and the Spirit against the flesh: and these are contrary the one to the other: so that ye cannot do the things that ye would."[203]

Paul continued:

"But the fruit of the Spirit is love, joy, peace, longsuffering, gentleness, goodness, faith, meekness, temperance: against such there is no law. Moreover, they that are Christ's have crucified the flesh with the affections and lusts. If we live in the Spirit, let us also walk in the Spirit."[204]

The Word of God commands us not to be drunk with wine, wherein there is excess, "but be filled with the Spirit; speaking to yourselves in psalms and hymns and spiritual songs, singing and making melody in your heart to the Lord; Giving thanks always for all things unto God and the Father in the name of our Lord Jesus Christ."[205] Jesus said, "For if I go not away, the Comforter will not come unto you; but if I depart, I will send Him unto you."[206] Here, Jesus spoke of the Holy Spirit whom He sent to be our counsellor, helper, advocate, intercessor, strength and comforter.

The moment we surrender our lives to Jesus Christ the Holy Spirit comes in and takes up residence in our hearts. He comes in to make us holy and to help us to live a life of practical holiness in a sinful world.

It is the Holy Spirit who gives us the desire to pray, the desire to know God, the hunger for holiness, a desire to be holy and the enabling power to overcome sin. If we are to fulfil God's mandate of holiness, we must allow the Holy Spirit to fill us to overflowing. Paul gave a practical code of conduct on how to live. He instructed us to "put off concerning the former conversation the old man, which is corrupt according to the deceitful lusts; and be renewed in the spirit of your mind, and we have to put on the new man, which after God is created in righteousness and true holiness."[207] Daily, moment by moment you must obey the Holy Spirit when He speaks to you and yield to Him when He guides. Nobody can do that for you.

Finally, you must be filled with the Holy Spirit, walk in the Holy Spirit and[18] "with all prayer and petition pray (with specific requests) always (on every occasion and in every season) in the Spirit, and with this in view, stay alert with all perseverance and petition (interceding in prayer) for all God's people."[208]

This I say to you:

"Trust in the LORD with all your heart and lean not on your understanding; in all your ways submit to Him, and He will make your paths straight. Do not be wise in your own eyes; fear the LORD and shun evil. This will bring health to your body and nourishment to your bones. "[209]

-PROVERBS 3: 5 - 8, NIV

The Holy Spirit is crucial in our lives. The anointing or filling with the Holy Spirit provides us with powerful and authoritative speech, (1 Corinthians 2:4, KJV). The Holy Spirit power enables the Christian: a) to be a witness for Jesus (Acts 1:8, KJV); b) to do great wonders and signs (Acts 6:8, KJV); c) to do good and heal (Acts 10:38, KJV); e) to abound in hope, (Romans 15:13, KJV); f) to speak and preach (1 Corinthians 2:45, KJV); g) to endure difficulties (2 Corinthians 6:6-10, KJV); h) to rejoice in weakness (2 Corinthians 12:9, KJV); i) to stand against the enemy in prayer (Ephesians 6:10, KJV); j) to be patient (Colossians 1:11, KJV); to be strengthened to know God's love (Ephesians 1:16,KJV), and to share in Christ's sufferings.

We must never forget that God the Holy Spirit is the third person of the Trinity. He is the Spirit of comfort; truth; wisdom; understanding and intelligence; counsel and advice; might and authority; knowledge and facts; and the reverence of the Lord. His goal is to bear fruit for Christ through us namely: to win souls (John 4:35,36, KJV), and Christlikeness (Galatians 5:22, 23, KJV).

Indeed, we can ask the Holy Spirit to descend upon our hearts at the Fountain Gate.

Spirit of God Descend Upon My Heart

1. Spirit of God descend upon my heart;
   Wean it from earth; through all its pulses move.
   Stoop to my weakness, mighty as Thou art,
   And make me love Thee as I ought to love.

2. Hast Thou not bid me love Thee, God and King?
   All, all Thine own, soul, heart and strength and mind.
   I see Thy cross; there teach my heart to cling:
   Oh, let me seek Thee, and, oh, let me find!

3. Teach me to feel that Thou art always nigh;
   Teach me the struggles of the soul to bear,
   To check the rising doubt, the rebel sigh;
   Teach me the patience of unanswered prayer

4. Teach me to love Thee as Thine angels love,
   One holy passion filling all my frame;
   The kindling of the heaven-descended Dove,
   My heart an altar, and Thy love the flame.

George Croly (1780-1860)

CHAPTER EIGHT

THE WATER GATE

*"Man shall not live by bread alone, but by every word that pro-
ceeds from the mouth of God."*[210] *(Mathew 4:3, KJV). "Let the
word of Christ dwell in you **richly** in all wisdom."*[211]

-COLOSSIANS 3:16A, KJV

Water is one of the most important substances on earth. All plants
and animals must have water to survive. If there were no water,
there would be no life on earth, for directly or indirectly, water affects all
facets of life. The Water Gate is the seventh gate in the Christian journey.
The **Sheep Gate** represented Jesus as the sacrificial Lamb of God who
died for us so that we can have eternal life. There, we received Jesus
Christ as our personal Saviour and Lord through faith and experienced
the new birth.[212] At the **Fish Gate**, we told our friends, family and the
world that Jesus saved us and shared our new life in Christ with them.

At the **Old Gate**, we consecrated our entire life to Christ and made
Jesus Lord of our lives. We then continued the long walk in holiness
through the valley to meet the **Valley Gate** that reminded us of all
the temptations, trials and tribulations and ups and downs that we had
experienced. At the Valley Gate, we remembered when our garden of
"Gethsemane" turned into an avalanche of suffering, betrayal and agony.

We were abandoned and burdened there, but through it all Jesus never left us. He was always there.

It was in the middle of the valley of "dry and very dry bones," when we were a seemingly useless, helpless and hopeless people, that God saved us by His grace even though we were dead in trespasses and sin. He vitalized and mobilized us and breathed life into us so that we could live again, speak again and walk again with God. He did not sleep. He did not slumber. He did not slack. He was with us in the valley.

Then at the **Dung Gate**, there was elimination; we put off the sins that so easily affected us. We then continued our journey and turned the corner towards the gates on the eastern wall. At the Fountain Gate, we filled the void that remained in us after **the purge** at the Dung Gate with, the Holy Spirit of God. We received more capacity to study and apply the Word of God, the power to witness and guidance to live. The Holy Spirit was the difference-maker.

Now we arrive at the **seventh gate**, the **Water Gate**. Seven is the number of perfection or completion. The Water Gate[213] led from the old City of David to the Gihon spring, located adjacent to the Kidron Valley. Jerusalem was not built near a great river, and the city depended on reservoirs and springs for its water. It is not a coincidence that the Water Gate was located next to the Fountain Gate, as the two often go together.

The Water Gate, therefore, is a picture of the Word of God and its effect on our lives. It was the temple servants living on the hill of Ophel (Mount Zion) who made repairs up to a point opposite the Water Gate towards the east and the projecting tower.[214]In Scripture, water represents the Word of God. We are washed by the water of the Word, and it is only through God's Word that we can be cleansed.[215]

Jesus told his disciples: *"Now ye are clean through the Word which I have spoken unto you. Abide in me, and I in you. As the branch cannot bear the fruit of itself, except it abide in the vine; no more can ye, except ye abide in me."*[216]

-JOHN 15:3–4, KJV

The writer of Hebrews told us:

"For the Word of God is living and powerful, and sharper than any two-edged sword, piercing even to the division of soul and spirit, and of joints and marrow, and is a discerner of the thoughts and intents of the heart."[217]

-HEBREWS 4:12, NKJV

Reading the Word of God is a command. "And Moses commanded them, saying: 'At the end of every seven years, in the solemnity of the year of release, in the feast of tabernacles, when all Israel is come to appear before the LORD thy God in the place which he shall choose, thou shalt read this law before all Israel in their hearing. Gather the people together, men and women, and children, and thy stranger that is within thy gates, that they may hear, and that they may learn, and fear the LORD your God, and observe to do all the words of this law:

And that their children, which have not known anything, may hear, and learn to fear the LORD your God, as long as *you* live in the land'"[218] (Deuteronomy 31:10–13, KJV).

After the completion of the wall around Jerusalem by Nehemiah, "... all the people assembled as one man in the square before the Water Gate. They told Ezra the scribe to bring out the Book of the Law of Moses, which the LORD had commanded for Israel. So, on the first day of the seventh month, Ezra the priest brought the Law before the assembly, which was made up of men and women and all who were able to understand. He read it aloud from daybreak till noon as he faced the square before the Water Gate in the presence of the men, women and others who could understand. And all the people listened attentively to the Book of the Law."[219]

The following are fourteen truths about the Word of God:

1. **It is tried.**

   As for God, his way is perfect; the word of the LORD is tried: he is a buckler to all them that trust in him.[220]

2. **It is pure.**

   The words of the LORD are pure words: as silver tried in a furnace of earth, purified seven times.[221]

3. **It cleans the ways of young men.**

   Wherewithal shall a young man cleanse his way? By taking heed of it according to thy word.[222]

4. **It runs very swiftly.**

   He sends forth his commandment upon earth: his word runs very swiftly.[223]

5. **It is food.**

   And he humbled thee, and suffered thee to hunger, and fed thee with manna, which thou knew not, neither did thy fathers know; that he might make thee know that man doth not live by bread only, but by every word that proceeded out of the mouth of the LORD doth man live.[224]

6. **It brings joy and rejoicing.**[225]

7. **It is trustworthy and profitable for instruction.**[226]

   It is better than the most exquisite gold and sweeter than honey. More to be desired are they than gold, yea, than much fine gold: sweeter also than honey and the honeycomb.[227]

8. **It furnishes light in the darkness.**

   - The statutes of the LORD are right, rejoicing the heart: the commandment of the LORD is pure, enlightening the eyes.[228]
   - Thy word is a lamp unto my feet, and a light unto my path. The word of God is a blessing to those who reverence it.[229]
   - For the LORD giveth wisdom: out of his mouth cometh knowledge and understanding.[230]
   - For the commandment is a lamp, and the law is light, and reproofs of instruction are the way of life.[231]
   - He was not that Light but was sent to bear witness of that Light.[232]

9. **It makes you wise.**

 - Therefore, whosoever hears these sayings of mine, and do them; I will liken him unto a wise man, which built his house upon a rock.[233]

 - But he said, yea rather, blessed are they that hear the word of God and keep it.[234] Then said Jesus to those Jews which believed on him, If ye continue in my word, then are ye my disciples indeed.[235]

10. **It sanctifies.**

 - Now ye are clean through the word which I have spoken unto you.[236]

 - Now they have known that all things whatsoever thou hast given me are of thee.[237] For it is sanctified by the word of God and prayer.[238]

11. **It is written with a purpose.**

 - But these are written, that ye might believe that Jesus is the Christ, the Son of God; and that believing ye might have life through his name.[239]

 - These things have I written unto you that believe on the name of the Son of God; that ye may know that ye have eternal life and that ye may believe on the name of the Son of God.[240]

12. **It is the standard of fault and duty.**

 - To the law and the testimony: if they speak not according to this word, it is because there is no light in them.[241]

 - For this cause also thank we God without ceasing, because, when ye received the word of God which ye heard of us, ye received it not as the word of men, but as it is in truth, the word of God, which effectually worketh also in you that believe.[242]

13. **It is the seed for the sower.**

 But he that received the seed into stony places, the same is he that heareth the word, and anon with joy receiveth it.[243]

14. **It is not to be altered.**

And if any man shall take away from the words of the book of this prophecy, God shall take away His part out of the book of life, and out of the holy city, and from the things which are written in this book.[244]

The Word of God is vital, for **faith *comes* by hearing**, and **hearing by** the Word of God.[245] It is our offensive weapon in spiritual warfare for it is the sword of the Spirit.[246]

Jesus spoke the Word of God when tempted in the wilderness. He responded three times. On the first occasion he said, **"It is written**, *'Man shall not live by bread alone, but by every word that proceeds from the mouth of God.'"*[247]

On the second occasion he said, *"It is written again, 'You shall not tempt the* LORD *your God.'"*[248]

On the third time he said, ' *"For it is written, 'You shall worship the* LORD *your God, and Him only you shall serve.'* Then the devil left Him, and behold, angels came and ministered to Him."[249]

Paul declared:

"For though we walk in the flesh, we do not war after the flesh: For the weapons of our warfare are not carnal, but mighty through God to the pulling down of strongholds; Casting down imaginations, and every high thing that exalts itself against the knowledge of God and bringing into captivity every thought to the obedience of Christ."[250]

-2 CORINTHIANS 10:3–5, KJV

Finally, the Water Gate preparation is vital for the warfare of the Christian at the Horse Gate and the getting through the East Gate. The word "water" is used in a variety of metaphorical ways in Scripture. Water speaks to us of physical (or natural) birth. Water speaks to us of the Word of God, (Ephesians 2:26; Psalm 119:9, KJV; John 15 :3, KJV). The Word of God has the piercing ability and operates with equal effectiveness unto sinners and saints. It is the sword of the Holy Spirit. Water is used to symbolize the troublesome times in life that can and do come to human beings, especially God's children (Psalm 32:6, KJV ; Psalms 69:1, KJV; Psalms 69:2, KJV; Psalms 69:14, KJV; Psalms 69:15, KJV ; Isaiah 43:2,KJV, and Lamentations 3:54, KJV).

In both the Old and New Testaments, the word "water" is used for salvation and eternal life, which God offers humankind through faith in his Son (Isaiah 12:3,KJV ; Isaiah55:1, KJV) ; Revelation 21:6, KJV ; Revelation 22:1, KJV Revelation 22:2, KJV; Revelation 22:17, KJV). In John 4:10-15, part of Jesus' discourse with the Samaritan woman at the well, He speaks metaphorically of his salvation as **"living water"** and as "a spring of water welling up to eternal life." Jesus answered and said to her, "Whoever drinks of this water will thirst again, but whoever drinks of the water that I shall give him will never thirst. But the water that I shall give him will become in him a fountain of water springing up into everlasting life" (John 4:1314, NKJV).

Twice in Jeremiah Yahweh is metaphorically identified as "the spring of living water" (Jeremiah 2:13; 17:13, KJV). In both instances, Israel is rebuked for having forsaken the Lord for other cisterns that could in no way satisfy their "thirst." In Revelation, Jesus affirms: "I am the Alpha and the Omega, the Beginning and the End. I will give of the fountain of the water of life freely to him who thirsts. He who overcomes shall inherit all things, and I will be his God, and he shall be My son (Revelation 21:6-7, NKJV).

Water sometimes symbolizes the spiritual cleansing that comes with the acceptance of God's offer of salvation (Ezekiel 36:25,KJV; Ephesians 5:26, KJV; Hebrews 10:22, KJV). Jesus identifies the "streams of living water" that flow from within those who believe in him with the Holy Spirit (John 7:37-39, KJV).

Water speaks to us of the purification of the Christian, (Ezekiel 36:25, KJV; Hebrews 10:22, KJV). Water was also crucial for **cleansing.**

Priests were washed at their consecration (Exodus 29:4, KJV), special ablutions were demanded for priests on the Day of Atonement (Leviticus 16:4, 24, 26, KJV) and of all men for the removal of ceremonial pollution (Leviticus 11:40, 15:15, KJV; Deuteronomy 23:11, KJV). The longing for water also indicates **spiritual need as** in Psalm 42:1, NKJV: "As the deer pants for the water brooks, so pants my soul for You, O God."

Water speaks to us of spiritual life, (Genesis 2:10; Exodus 17:6; Isaiah 12:23; 55:1; Jeremiah 2:13; John 4:14, John 7:38-39; Revelation 22:12,17). In Genesis chapter two we read of the perfect conditions of the garden of Eden. This garden was watered by a river (Genesis 2:10, KJV). Without water, the garden would have died, as plants, animals and humans cannot survive without water. This river is a beautiful picture of the life that Christ gives to His children through the Spirit of God.

Water is also symbolic of God's **blessing** and **spiritual refreshment.** *"for in the wilderness shall waters break out, and streams in the desert. And the parched ground shall become a pool and the thirsty land springs of water"* (Isaiah 35:6-7, KJV). *When the poor and needy seek water, and there is none, and their tongue faileth for thirst, I the LORD will hear them, I the God of Israel will not forsake them. I will open rivers in high places, and fountains in the midst of the valleys: I will make the wilderness a pool of water, and the dry land springs of water* (Isaiah 41:17-18, KJV). In Ezekiel's vision of God's house, the waters that poured from under the threshold represented the unrestricted flow of God's **blessings** upon his people (Ezekiel 47:1-12, KJV). Jeremiah describes **God** as " the fountain of living waters" (Jeremiah 2:13, 17:13, KJV).

Let us remember that there is a **crown of glory** that will be given to faithful preachers and teachers of the Word of God, (Acts 20:26-28, KJV; 2 Timothy 4:1, 2, KJV; 1Peter 5:2-4, NKJV). So, let us obey the admonition of the Apostle Peter:

*"Shepherd the flock of God which is among you, serving as over-seers, not by compulsion but willingly, not for dishonest gain but eagerly; nor as being lords over those entrusted to you, but being examples to the flock; and when the Chief Shepherd appears, you will receive the **crown of glory** that does not fade away."*

-1 PETER 5:2-4, NKJV

To go through the Horse Gate, the Word of God is indispensable. Be strengthened by the words of the psalmist and the hymn "Wonderful Words of Life."

The Law of the Lord

The law of the Lord is perfect, converting the soul:
The testimony of the Lord is sure, making wise the simple.
More to be desired are they than gold, yea, than much fine gold:
Sweeter also than honey and the honeycomb.

The statutes of the Lord are right, rejoicing the heart:
The commandment of the Lord is pure, enlightening the eyes.
More to be desired are they than gold, yea, than much fine gold:
Sweeter also than honey and the honeycomb.

The fear of the Lord is clean, enduring forever:
The judgments of the Lord are true and righteous together.
More to be desired are they than gold, yea,
than much fine gold: sweeter also than honey and the honeycomb.

Moreover, by them is thy servant warned:
And in the keeping of them, there is great reward.
More to be desired are they than gold, yea, than much fine gold:
sweeter also than honey and the honeycomb.[251]

-PSALM 19:7-11, KJV

Wonderful Words of Life

1. Sing them over again to me,
   Wonderful words of life,
   Let me more of their beauty see,
   Wonderful words of life;
   Words of life and beauty
   Teach me faith and duty.

   Refrain:
   Beautiful words, wonderful words,
   Wonderful words of life;
   Beautiful words, wonderful words,
   Wonderful words of life.

2. Christ, the Blessed One gives to all
   Wonderful words of life;
   Sinner, list to the loving call,
   Wonderful words of life;
   All so freely given,
   Wooing us to heaven.

3. Sweetly echo the Gospel call,
   Wonderful words of life;
   Offer pardon and peace to all,
   Wonderful words of life;
   Jesus, only Saviour,
   Sanctify us forever.

Philip Paul Bliss (1838-1876)

CHAPTER NINE

THE HORSE GATE

"Finally, my brethren, be strong in the Lord and in the power of His might. Put on the whole armour of God, that you may be able to stand against the wiles of the devil."[252]

-EPHESIANS 6:10–11, KJV

The Horse Gate[253] was north of the Water Gate. It was adjacent to the temple area and was south-east of the temple, near the city of David, which initially was the Jebusite fortress.[254] The gate was so named perhaps because of the many horses connected with the kings of Israel and with the city of David. Horses are always referred to in the Bible in connection with warlike operations, except in Isaiah 28:28. The warhorse is described in Job 39:19–25. The horse, therefore, is the symbol of battle in Scripture. The Horse Gate speaks to us of warfare. This gate was not destroyed in the past battles and assures us that in all these things we are more than conquerors.[255]

In the book of Revelation, John said:

"And I saw Heaven opened and behold a white horse, and he that sat upon him was called Faithful and True, and in righteousness he doth judge and make war."[256]

Spiritual warfare is resisting, overcoming and defeating the enemy's deceptions, temptations and accusations that he sends our way. It is a battle that one must wrestle with **spiritual** wickedness, and this **warfare** is not one of flesh and blood. It is a battle against the "dark side," no matter where it lies. Spiritual warfare was the big battle in the rebuilding of the wall around Jerusalem.

The Scriptures have provided us with all the required weapons to fight these battles. Some of the provisions are as follows:

▶ When thou goest out to battle against thine enemies, and seest horses, and chariots, and a people more than thou, be not afraid of them: for the Lord thy God is with thee, which brought thee up out of the land of Egypt.[257]

▶ He that dwelleth in the secret place of the Most High shall abide in under the shadow of the Almighty. I will say of the Lord, He is my refuge and my fortress: my God; in him will I trust. Surely, he shall deliver thee from the snare of the fowler, and from the noisome pestilence. He shall cover thee with his feathers, and under his wings shalt thou trust: his truth shall be thy shield and buckler. Thou shalt not be afraid or the terror by night; nor for the arrow that flieth by day.[258]

▶ Be sober-minded; be watchful. Your adversary, the devil, prowls around like a roaring lion, seeking someone to devour.[259] Submit yourselves therefore to God. Resist the devil, and he will flee from you.[260]

▶ The Lord will cause your enemies who rise against you to be defeated before you. They shall come out against you one way and flee before you seven ways.[261]

▶ No weapon that is formed against thee shall prosper; and every tongue that shall rise against thee in judgment thou shalt condemn. This is the heritage of the servants of the Lord, and their vindication is righteousness is of me, saith the Lord.[262]

▸ In all these things, we are more than conquerors through Him who loved us.[263]

▸ But thanks be to God, who gives us the victory through our Lord Jesus Christ.[264]

▸ But the Lord is faithful, and he will strengthen you and protect you from the evil one.[265]

In his writings to the Ephesians, Paul provided solutions for how we are to fight spiritual warfare.[266] It was written for all of us by the apostle Paul in the Book of books. The following are his strategies to overcome in spiritual warfare:

1. We must be strong in the Lord,[267]

strong for service, strong for suffering and strong for fighting. Spiritual strength and courage are essential for our spiritual warfare. We have no sufficient strength of our own. Our natural courage is as absolute cowardice, and our physical strength as perfect weakness, but all our sufficiency is of God. In His strength, we must go forth and go on. We must resist temptations and rely upon God's all-sufficiency and the omnipotence of His might.

2. We must be well armed:

"Put on the whole armour of God."[268] We must make use of all the weapons for repelling the temptations and ploys of the enemy. We must put on the whole armour of God and ensure that no part is exposed to the enemy. We do not need any other armour, and no substitute must be used. This armour was prepared for us, but we must put it on and use it that we may be able to hold out and to overcome, withstanding all of the devil's assaults, all of the deceits he puts upon us, all of the snares he lays for us and all of his conspiracies against us.

The enemy is the devil and all the powers of darkness. The combat for which we are to be prepared is not against ordinary human enemies, not against *flesh and blood*, but against the several ranks of devils who have a government that they control in this world. We are up against a subtle enemy, an enemy who uses wiles and stratagems. He has a thousand ways of beguiling unstable souls; hence he is called a serpent for subtlety, an old serpent, experienced in the art and trade of tempting.

He is a powerful enemy: *principalities*, and *powers*, and *rulers*. They are numerous; they are vigorous. They are spiritual enemies: *spiritual wickedness in high places*, or wicked spirits, as some translate it. The devil is a spirit, a wicked spirit, and our danger is great because they are unseen and assault us when we are unaware of them. Our duty is to take up and put on the whole armour of God, and then to stand our ground and withstand our enemies.

3. We must *withstand*.[269]

We must not yield to the devil's allurements and assaults, but oppose them. We must stand against him, and be sober and vigilant and alert at all times. He is the wicked one, and his kingdom is the kingdom of sin. To stand against the devil is to strive against sin, *that you may be able to withstand in the evil day*, in the day of temptation.

4. We must stand our ground.[270]

We must resolve, by God's grace, not to yield to the devil. Resist him, and he will flee. Our present business is to withstand the assaults of the devil, and to stand it out, and then, having done all that is incumbent on us as good soldiers of Jesus Christ, our warfare will be accomplished and we shall be finally victorious.

5. We must stand armed, with complete armour.

The armour is divine. It is the *armour of God, the armour of light.*[271] It is the *armour of righteousness.*[272] The armour is both offensive and defensive – that is the belt, the breastplate, the soldier's shoes, the shield, the helmet, and the sword. It is observable that among them all there is none for the back; if we turn our back upon the enemy, we lie exposed. Truth or sincerity is our girdle.[273] It was prophesied of Christ that *righteousness should be the girdle of his loins and faithfulness the girdle of his reins.*[274] Righteousness must be our breastplate.

The breastplate secures the vitals, shelters the heart. *Put on the breastplate of faith and love,*[275] for by faith we are united to Christ and by love to our brethren.

6.   *Our feet must be shod with the preparation of the gospel of peace.*[276]
The preparation of the gospel of peace signifies a prepared and resolved frame of heart, to adhere to the gospel and abide by it, which will enable us to walk with a steady pace, notwithstanding the difficulties and dangers that we may face. It is called *the gospel of peace* because it brings all sorts of peace – peace with God, with ourselves, and with one another.

7.   Faith must be our shield: *Above all, taking the shield of faith.*[277]
Faith is all in all to us in an hour of temptation. The breastplate secures the vitals, but with the shield, we can turn every way. *This is the victory over the world, even our faith.* Consider faith as it *is the evidence of things not seen and the substance of things hoped for,*[278] and it will be of effective use in warfare. Faith is the shield with which we must quench all the fiery darts of the devil that they may not hit us, or at least that they may not hurt us. We must have dynamic faith that banishes fear, for fear and faith cannot reside together. Dynamic faith is faith that is real, faith that has power, faith that results in a changed life. Dynamic faith is based on God's Word, and *it involves the whole man.*

In warfare we must trust in God and be able to say,

"Behold, God is my salvation; I will trust, and not be afraid: for the LORD JEHOVAH *is my strength and my song; he also is become my salvation."*[279]

8. Salvation must be our helmet.[280]

The helmet secures the head. The head supports the face and is maintained by the skull, which itself encloses the brain. The mind is the target of the devil. We must guard our mind; God must control it. We must "grow in grace and the knowledge of our Lord and Saviour Jesus Christ."[281] Paul declared, "Let this mind be in you which was also in Christ Jesus;[282] and do not be conformed to this world, but be transformed by the renewing of your mind, that you may prove what *that good and acceptable and perfect will of God is.*"[283]

9. We must watch and pray.

When Nehemiah was rebuilding the wall around Jerusalem, and the enemy was trying to stop the work, he defeated them by watching and praying. Nevertheless, we made our prayer unto our God and set a watch.[284] Watching and praying are the secrets to victory over the world,[285] the flesh[286] and the devil.[287] When God says *seek my face*, our hearts must comply.[288] We must pray *with all perseverance*, and we must pray *with supplication*, not for ourselves only, but *for all saints*; for we are members, one of another. At the Horse Gate, we dare not quit, for quitters never win. We must fight the good fight of faith. Lay hold on eternal life. Fear not.

Exodus chapter seventeen records that a few weeks had elapsed from the time the children of Israel left Marah, the place of bitter waters, till they reached Rephidim, Israel discovered that there were worse enemies than even hunger and thirst. For "then came Amalek and fought with Israel in Rephidim" (Exodus 17:8, KJV). Moses went upon a hill with the rod of God, in his hand, which was a symbol of the presence and power of God. In the account we are told that when Moses held up his hand or his hand was held up, Israel prevailed, and when his hand was lowered Amalek prevailed. Israel finally defeated the Amalekites. The rod in Moses' hand was the symbol and pledge of God's presence, power and working. **Moses called the name of the altar which he built there Jehovah-nissi--Jehovah, Himself, is my banner.**

Jehovah-nissi teaches us that we cannot fight this warfare in our own strength alone. The evil forces of the world are powerful and implacable, too great for man's own, unaided strength, *but* the banner of Jehovah held aloft in Moses' upraised hand brought victory to His people. Victory is always assured to the people of God over the powers of evil and the enemy of our souls when His banner is over us.

The cross of Jesus Christ is our banner of God's mighty power in redemption. He is also the banner of our warfare. He has conquered before us; "in the world, ye shall have tribulation: but be of good cheer; I have overcome the world" (John 16:33). He, too, promises His presence. "Lo, I am with you always even unto the end of the world" (Matthew 28:20, KJV). Faith in Him is the assurance of our victory, for "this is the victory that overcometh the world, even our faith" (1 John 5:4). Our faith is in Him whom Paul tells us has been placed far above all principality, and power, and might, and dominion, and every name that is named in this age and in the age to come (Ephesians 1:19-22, KJV), so that in Him we will be able to wrestle against those principalities and powers of evil successfully.

We cannot defeat the devil in our own strength or by human intellect or cleverness. James admonishes us to resist the devil and he will flee and draw near to God and He will draw near to you. Defeating the devil is the work of Jesus Christ alone, and that work was accomplished on the cross. The war has already been won. We are therefore assured that: "If God be for us, who can be against us?" For "we are more than conquerors through him that loved us," (Romans 8:31, 37, KJV). Jesus is our banner. Thus we shall go from strength to strength with each victory, and we must say: "Thanks be to God, which giveth us the victory through our Lord Jesus Christ.

Be courageous and keep the faith. God is our refuge and strength, a very present help in trouble.[289] We can, therefore, sing "**Sound the Battle Cry**" as we march towards the East Gate looking up.

Sound the Battle Cry

1. *Sound the battle cry! See, the foe is nigh;*
   Raise the standard high for the Lord;
   Gird your armour on, stand firm every one;
   Rest your cause upon His holy Word.

   Refrain:
   Rouse, then, soldiers, rally round the banner,
   Ready, steady, pass the word along;
   Onward, forward, shout aloud, "Hosanna!"
   Christ is Captain of the mighty throng.

2. *Strong to meet the foe, marching on we go,*
   While our cause we know must prevail;
   Shield and banner bright, gleaming in the light,
   Battling for the right we ne'er can fail.

   Refrain:
   Rouse, then, soldiers, rally round the banner,
   Ready, steady, pass the word along;
   Onward, forward, shout aloud, "Hosanna!"
   Christ is Captain of the mighty throng.

3. *O Thou God of all, hear us when we call,*
   Help us one and all by Thy grace;
   When the battle's done, and the victory's won,
   May we wear the crown before Thy face.

William F. Sherwin, (1826-1888)

CHAPTER TEN

THE EAST GATE

"Watch, therefore, for you do not know what hour your Lord is coming. Therefore, you also be ready, for the Son of Man is coming at an hour you do not expect."[290]

-MATHEW 24:42, 44, NKJV

The East Gate[291] needed no repairs. It was the middle of the three gates that led into the temple compound, the other two being the Water Gate and the Inspection Gate. This gate had a particular prophetic significance for the people of Israel[292] and represented the coming of the Glory of the Lord,[293] and both the first coming of the Lord of Glory[294] and the second coming.[295] The East Gate opened and looked towards the Mount of Olives. The week before His crucifixion, Jesus spent much time there. He also went through the East Gate,[296] and He ascended to heaven from the Mount of Olives.[297] When Jesus returns, He will return to this mount.[298] He will again pass through the East Gate and into the city of Jerusalem.[299]

The prophet declared:

"...the gate that looked toward the east, and it was shut. And the Lord said to me, "This gate shall be shut; it shall not be opened, and no man shall enter by it, because the Lord God of Israel has entered by it; therefore it shall be shut."[300]

The East Gate, therefore, speaks of the return of Jesus Christ and shows us our need to live with hope and to long for His return. In his exhortation to the Thessalonians,

Paul declared:

"But I do not want you to be ignorant, brethren, concerning those who have fallen asleep, lest you sorrow as others who have no hope. For if we believe that Jesus died and rose again, even so, God will bring with Him those who sleep in Jesus. For this, we say to you by the word of the Lord, that we who are alive and remain until the coming of the Lord will by no means precede those who are asleep. For the Lord, Himself will descend from heaven with a shout, with the voice of an archangel, and with the trumpet of God. And the dead in Christ will rise first. Then we who are alive and remain shall be caught up together with them in the clouds to meet the Lord in the air. And thus, we shall always be with the Lord. Therefore comfort one another with these words."[301]

-1 THESSALONIANS 4:13–18, NKJV

The events of the rapture can be summarized as follows:

1. The Lord Himself will descend from His Father's house, where He is preparing a place for us.[302]
2. He will come again to receive us to Himself.[303]

3. He resurrects those who have fallen asleep in Him (deceased believers whom we will not precede).[304]

4. The Lord shouts as He descends.[305] All this takes place in the "twinkling of an eye."[306]

5. We will hear the voice of the archangel.[307]

6. We will also hear the trumpet call of God,[308] His last trumpet for the church.

7. The dead in Christ will rise first.[309]

8. Then we who are alive and remain shall be changed, (made incorruptible by having our bodies made "immortal").[310]

9. Then we shall be caught up (raptured) together[311] with them in the clouds (where dead and living believers will have a monumental reunion).[312]

10. We will meet the Lord in the air.[313]

11. To "receive you to myself": Jesus will bring us to the Father's house "that where I am, there you may also be."[314]

12. "And so shall we ever be with the Lord."[315]

13. At the judgment seat of Christ all Christians will have to give an account of their total lives to Christ. "We must all appear before the judgment seat of Christ, so that each of us may receive what is due us for the things done while in the body, whether good or bad."[316] He will judge all things. Christians will be rewarded based on how faithfully they served Christ (1 Corinthians 9:4-27; 2 Timothy 2:5)[317, 318]

14. This judgment will prepare Christians for the marriage supper of the Lamb. Just before His coming to earth in power and great glory, Christ will meet His bride, the church, and the marriage supper will take place. In the meantime, after the church is raptured, the world will suffer the unprecedented time of the wrath of God, which our Lord called the great tribulation.[319]

My advice to you is that at the **East Gate** be a watcher, for Christ may come at any time, and you must be ready. You must watch for Christ, for this hope has a purifying effect.[320] You must watch for Christ for it is an indication of your faithfulness.[321] Watching for Christ will bring blessings now and rewards in eternity.[322] Paul declared: *"Henceforth there is laid up for me a **crown of righteousness**, which the Lord, the righteous judge, shall give me at that day: and not to me only, but unto all them also that love his appearing"*[323] *(2 Timothy 4:8, KJV).*

Titus told us:

"For the grace of God that brings salvation has appeared to all men, teaching us that, denying ungodliness and worldly lusts, we should live soberly, righteously, and godly in the present age, looking for the blessed hope and glorious appearing of our great God and Saviour Jesus Christ."[324]

-TITUS 2:11–13, NKJV

Therefore, during this in between time while we are watching and waiting for the appearing of our Lord Jesus we must: a) not forsake the assembling of ourselves for worship (Hebrews 10:25. KJV); b) love one another (1 Thessalonians 3: 12,13, KJV); c) be patient (James 5:8, KJV); d) observe the Lord's Supper with the rapture in mind (Corinthians11:2, KJV); e) live a separated life (1 John3:2,3, KJV; Titus 2:12,13, KJV; 1John2:28, KJV); f) refrain from judging others (1Corinthians 4:5, KJV); g) preach the Word of God (2 Timothy 4: 1,2, KJV); 1Peter 5:2,4, KJV); h) comfort the bereaved (1Thessalonians 4: 16, 18, KJV); i) win souls for Christ (Jude 21-23, KJV), and j) be concerned with heaven (Colossians 3:14, KJV).

In summary, we who are alive at His coming shall meet the Lord in the air, in person, when He comes for us. We have lived for Christ by faith here on earth, but in the air, we shall "see him as he is" and become like Him (1 John 3:1–2, KJV). It will be a *great* meeting because we shall have glorified bodies.

Remember when He was here on earth, Jesus prayed that we might one day see His glory and share in it (John 17:22–24, KJV). The suffering that we endured during our journey on earth will be transformed into glory when Christ returns (Romans 8:17–19, KJV; 2 Corinthians. 4:17–18, KJV). It will be an *everlasting* meeting, for we shall be "forever with the Lord." This was His promise: "I will come again and receive you unto myself; that where I am, there ye may be also" (John 14:3, KJV). God always keeps His promises. Our meeting with the Lord will also be a time of *reckoning*. Our works will be judged, and rewards will be given (1 Corinthians 3:8–15, KJV). Let us live our lives so that when He appears, we who are alive will be caught up to meet Him in the air. Let the hymn "When the roll is call up yonder" be our song of praise.

When the Roll Is Called Up Yonder

1. When the trumpet of the Lord shall sound,
   and time shall be no more,
   and the morning breaks, eternal, bright and fair;
   when the saved of earth shall gather over on the other shore,
   and the roll is called up yonder; I'll be there.

   Refrain:
   When the roll is called up yonder,
   when the roll is called up yonder,
   when the roll is called up yonder,
   when the roll is called up yonder, I'll be there.

2. On that bright and cloudless morning
   when the dead in Christ shall rise,
   and the glory of his resurrection share;
   when his chosen ones shall gather
   to their home beyond the skies,
   and the roll is called up yonder, I'll be there.

   (Refrain)

3. Let us labour for the Master from the dawn till setting sun,
   let us talk of all his wondrous love and care;
   then when all of life is over, and our work on earth is done, and
   the roll is called up yonder, I'll be there.

   Refrain:

   When the roll is called up yonder,
   when the roll is called up yonder,
   when the roll is called up yonder,
   when the roll is called up yonder, I'll be there.

James M. Black (1856-1938)

CHAPTER ELEVEN

THE INSPECTION GATE

*"For we shall all stand before the judgment seat of Christ. So
then each of us shall give an account of himself to God."*[325]

-ROMANS 14:10B, 12, KJV

The Inspection Gate[326] is the final gate in the walk of the Christian.
The Hebrew word used for this gate's name is *Miphkad*, which can
be translated as "appointment, mandate, designated spot, mustering, the
numbering in a census." For this reason, this gate has the following three
common names: a)the Inspection Gate, b) the Muster Gate and c) the
Gate *Miphkad*. This gate led into the temple courtyard, the "appointed
place" of God's presence. It is the gate through which we must pass when
we die. The psalmist declared, "LORD, make me know my end, and the
measure of my days, what it is: that I may know how frail I am,"[327]and
the writer of Hebrews said, "And as it is appointed to men once to die,
but after this the judgment."[328]

This gate speaks to us of the examination of our lives by the Lord.
Matthew reminded us that, "When the Son of man shall come in his
glory, and all the holy angels with him, then shall he sit upon the throne
of his glory and before him shall be gathered all nations: and he shall
separate them one from another, as a shepherd divides his sheep from

the goats and he shall set the sheep on his right hand, but the goats on the left."[329]

The apostle Peter admonished us that, 'The Lord is not slack concerning his promise, as some men count slackness; but is longsuffering to us-ward, not willing that any should perish, but that all should come to repentance.'[330] Why would God see it important to remind us of the final judgment? Because He hopes it will motivate us to desire the label "sheep"! Remember: *"He is patient with you, not wanting anyone to perish, but everyone to come to repentance."*[331] We are told that the kingdom of Heaven should be looked at like a treasure:

> *"The kingdom of heaven is like treasure hidden in a field. When a man found it, he hid it again, and then in his joy went and sold all he had and bought that field. Again, the kingdom of heaven is like a merchant looking for fine pearls. When he found one of immense value, he went away and sold everything he had and bought it"*[332].
>
> *(MATTHEW 13:44–46, NIV)*

Jesus also admonishes us: to store up our treasures in heaven, not on earth: *"sell your possessions and give to the poor, provide purses for yourselves that will not wear out, a treasure in heaven that will not be exhausted, where no thief comes near, and no moth destroys, for where your treasure is, there your heart will also be"*[333] *(Luke 12:33–34, NIV).* This theme is further carried out by Paul in his letter to Timothy when he declared: *"Command them to do good, to be rich in good deeds, and to be generous and willing to share. in this way, they will lay up treasure for themselves as a firm foundation for the coming age, so that they may take hold of the life that is truly life.[334] For we must all appear before the judgment seat of Christ; that every one may receive the things done in his body, according to that he hath done, whether it be **good or bad**"*[335] *(2 Corinthians 5:10, KJV).*

This Inspection Gate once again calls us to live our lives with eternity in view. The entire Christian walk, starting with salvation, all leads up to one cumulative point: we must learn to care more for the things of eternity than for the temporal things that we see around us.[336] It reminds us that we are called to live our lives with eternity in view, for in so doing, we lay up our treasure in heaven where no thief comes near, and no moth destroys. The Church of Jesus Christ will rejoice at the Inspection Gate and will sweep through the pearly gates of the new Jerusalem. I ask you this question: Are you **ready** for the Judgment Day?

1. There's a great day coming, a great day coming,
   There's a great day coming by and by;
   When the saints and the sinners shall be parted right and left, are you ready for that day to come?

   Chorus:
   Are you ready? Are you ready?
   Are you ready for the judgment day?
   Are you ready? Are you ready?
   For the judgment day?

2. There's a bright day coming, a bright day coming,
   There's a bright day coming by and by;
   But its brightness shall only come to them that love the Lord, are you ready for that day to come?

   (Chorus)

3. There's a sad day coming, A sad day coming,
   There's a sad day coming by and by;
   When the sinner shall hear his doom,
   "Depart, I know you not,"
   Are you ready for that day to come?

Will L. Thompson (1847-1909)

He the Pearly Gates will Open

1. Love divine, so great and wondrous,
   Deep and mighty, pure, sublime!
   Coming from the heart of Jesus,
   Just the same through tests of time.

   Refrain
   He the pearly gates will open,
   So that I may enter in;
   For He purchased my redemption,
   and forgave me all my sin.

2. Like a dove when hunted, frightened,
   As a wounded fawn was I;
   Brokenhearted, yet He healed me,
   He will heed the sinner's cry.

   Refrain

3. Love divine, so great and wondrous,
   All my sins He then forgave!
   I will sing His praise forever,
   For His blood, His power to save.

   Refrain

4. In life's eventide, at twilight,
   At His door I'll knock and wait;
   By the precious love of Jesus
   I shall enter Heaven's gate.

   Refrain

Fredrick A. Blom (1879-1927) translated from Swedish to English by Nathaniel Carlson, *circa* 1935

CHAPTER TWELVE

THE GATE OF EPHRAIM

*"And if you are Christ's, then you are Abraham's **seed**, and heirs according to the promise."*[337]

-GALATIANS 3:29, KJV

The Gate of Ephraim[338] was mentioned by Nehemiah after the project was completed. It was named after Joseph's last son Ephraim. Joseph, the eleventh son of Jacob, was the first son and child of Jacob's beloved wife Rachael.[339] The record of his life presents him as being flawless. He is undoubtedly among the most outstanding characters of the Bible. The account of his marvellous life covers almost fourteen full chapters. In some chapters or narrative concentration, the recorded history of Joseph is much longer than that of Isaac and Jacob, or even of Abraham. Jacob was very fond of Joseph's sons. He kissed them and embraced them.[340] Solomon declared, "Children's children are the crown of old men, and the glory of children are their fathers."[341]

When Joseph was told that his father was sick, he took his two sons, Manasseh and Ephraim, to Jacob. Israel (Jacob) strengthened himself and sat upon the bed.[342] And Israel beheld Joseph's sons and said, who are these? Joseph said unto his father, they are my sons, whom God hath given me in this place. He said, bring them, I pray thee, unto me, and I will bless them. And he brought them near unto him, and he kissed them and embraced them. And Israel said unto Joseph; God hath showed me your seed.[343]

Before giving his blessings, Jacob recounted his experiences of God's goodness when God appeared to him.[344] He shared God's grace, and the special communion he had with Him was not forgotten. He talked about the constant care of God for him throughout his life,[345] how God had fed him all his life long unto this day.[346] He talked about a great deal of hardship in his time, and how God had graciously kept him from the evil of his troubles.

When Joseph saw that his father laid his right hand upon the head of Ephraim, it displeased him: and he held up his father's hand, to remove it from Ephraim's head unto Manasseh's head. Joseph said unto his father, not so, my father: for this is the firstborn; put thy right hand upon his head. And his father refused, and said, I know it, my son, I know it: he also shall become a people, and he also shall be great: but truly his younger brother shall be greater than he, and his seed shall become a multitude of nations. And he blessed them that day, saying, in thee shall Israel be blessed, God make thee as Ephraim and as Manasseh: and he set Ephraim before Manasseh.[347]

The **Gate of Ephraim** teaches us the following:

1) In our old age, we should witness for our God: that we have found Him gracious; that the experiences of God's goodness improve daily; that we have great satisfaction living for him. This should be done both to encourage others to serve God and to encourage ourselves to bless and pray for others.

2) Those who would inherit the blessings of their godly parents, and have the benefit of God's covenant with them, must walk in the steps of their righteousness and service to God.

3) God, in his merciful providences, exceeds our expectations and greatly magnifies His favours.

4) There are greatness and multiple growths of nations for the children and grandchildren who inherit God's blessings from godly grandparents.

5) God not only prevents our fears but exceeds our hopes.

6) God shows our seed to our grandparents who are in covenant with Him.

7) In bestowing His blessings upon his people, God gives more to some than to others – more gifts, graces, comforts and more of the good things of this life.

8) God often gives most to those who are the least. He chooses the weak things of the world to confound the wise; raises the poor out of the dust. Grace observes not the order of nature, nor does God prefer those whom we think fittest to be preferred, but does as it pleases Him.

9) It is observable how often God, by the distinguishing favours of His covenant, advanced the younger above the elder: Abel above Cain, Shem above Japheth, Abraham above Nahor and Haran, Isaac above Ishmael, Jacob above Esau; Judah and Joseph were preferred before Reuben, Moses before Aaron, David and Solomon before their elder brethren.

"But the LORD said unto Samuel, Do not look at his appearance, or at his physical stature; because I have refused him. For the Lord does not see as man sees; for man looks at the outward appearance, but the Lord looks at the heart."[348]

-1 SAMUEL 16:7, NKJV

10. There is power and great significance in the blessings of godly grandfathers. Never despise their blessings.

Let us sing the hymn "Faith of our Fathers" in their honour.

Faith of Our Fathers

1. *Faith of our Fathers! living still*
   In spite of dungeon, fire, and sword:
   Oh, how our hearts beat high with joy
   Whene'er we hear that glorious word.
   Faith of our Fathers! Holy Faith!
   We will be true to thee till death.

2. *Our Fathers, chained in prisons dark,*
   Were still in heart and conscience free:
   How sweet would be their children's fate
   If they, like them, could die for thee!
   Faith of our Fathers! Holy Faith!
   We will be true to thee till death.

3. *Faith of our Fathers! We will strive*
   To win all nations back to thee:
   And through the truth that comes from God
   Mankind shall then indeed be free.
   Faith of our Fathers! Holy Faith!
   We will be true to thee till death

4. *Faith of our Fathers! we will love*
   Both friend and foe in all our strife:
   And preach thee too, as love knows how
   By kindly words and virtuous life:
   Faith of our Fathers! Holy Faith!
   We will be true to thee till death

Frederick William Faber (1814–1863)

CHAPTER THIRTEEN

THE PRISON GATE

"For God did not send His Son into the world to condemn the world, but that the world through Him might be saved. He who believes in Him is not condemned, but he who does not believe is condemned already because he has not believed in the name of the only begotten Son of God."[349]

-JOHN 3:17–18, NKJV

The Prison Gate[350] was located to the right of the Sheep Gate and to the left of the Inspection Gate. It was where the two processions stood still and gave thanks before entering the temple during the dedication ceremony of the completed wall around Jerusalem. It was the gate where the prisoners entered the prison. It is not a gate for the Christian to enter. The existence of the prison gate raises the question: **Is there a hell to shun?** The saddest story in the Bible tells of a certain rich man who died and was buried. And being in torment in hell, he cried and said, "Father Abraham, have mercy on me." But Abraham said, "Between us and you there is a great gulf fixed so that those who want to pass from here to you cannot, nor can those from there pass to us."[351]

In the story, Jesus shows us how life in eternity is determined by the life we live on earth and he revealed the conversations of two men after they had died. One man lived for God despite adverse circumstances and was carried into heaven. The other man lived for self despite all his privileges and opportunities, and is found tormented in hell. Jesus showed how relevant and personal this question is: Is there a hell, a hell to shun?

The story teaches us about the fact of hell, the rich man died and was buried, and in Hades, he cried.[352] Jesus confronts us with the inescapable fact of hell. Notice that hell has to do with *the fact of a* person whose indifference, indulgence and infidelity resulted in his death without God and hope. Then he reappears in hell with a capacity to see and recognize persons, hear, speak, feel and remember. He had a tongue, eyes, memory, intelligence, feelings, emotions, will, voice, and reasoning powers. The nameless rich man had five brothers, and the poor man was given a proper name: Lazarus. Jesus was driving home the fact that hell is personal, and this story is about you and me.

Hell has to do with *the fact of a place*. "In Hades, he cried." Whether this is a location or a condition or both is not the central issue. Jesus spoke of hell as a place to establish the fact. It is an unseen realm, for that is the meaning of the word *hades* or hell. It is a state that is associated with suffering because the rich man in the story calls it "this place of torment."[353] It is a sphere into which souls pass after death. What is more critical and manifestly clear, however, is that hell is a fact.

There is also the flame of hell. The rich man declared:"I am tormented in this flame."[354] These are terrifying words but are nonetheless truthful. They reveal the horrors that await those who choose to go to hell. From Jesus' own words, the torments of hell result from the flame of an uncleansed conscience: "Son, remember that in your lifetime you received your good things."[355]

This rich man had received all the "good things" of life without a thought for God. However, even with this knowledge, he chose to leave God out of his life. He deliberately and defiantly committed the spiritual sin that damns men's souls. The torments of hell resulted from the flame of an unsatisfied capacity. "Then he cried and said, 'Father Abraham, have mercy on me, and send Lazarus that he may dip the tip of his finger in water and cool my tongue.'"[356] This man had lived a life for self-gratification and created and developed a capacity that nothing but his tongue could satisfy, but now there was not even a drop of water to satisfy the craving void of an unsatisfied capacity. The torments of hell further result from the flame of an unrelieved concern: "I have five brothers."[357]

This man never cared for his brothers until he was in hell, but now the flame of unfulfilled social obligations exposed his sins. He realized the truth of the saying, "None of us lives to himself, and no one dies to himself."[358]

The story also communicates to us the finality of hell: "'Now, you are tormented,' said Abraham. 'And besides all this, between you and us there is a great gulf fixed.'"[359] It teaches the finality of hell's *sentence*: "Now you are tormented."[360] This sentence is final. Examine, for example, the following warnings about hell in scripture, and you will find that in every instance the sentence is always expressed in words that denote finality. "And these will go away into everlasting punishment."[361]

There is nothing revocable about that sentence. It is final. Jesus said, "Fear Him who is able to destroy both soul and body in hell."[362]

Paul declared:

"and to give you who are troubled rest with us when the Lord Jesus is revealed from heaven with His mighty angels, in flaming fire taking vengeance on those who do not know God, and on those who do not obey the gospel of our Lord Jesus Christ. These shall be punished with everlasting destruction from the presence of the Lord and from the glory of His power, when He comes, in that Day, to be glorified in His saints and to be admired among all those who believe."[363]

-2 THESSALONIANS 1:7–10, NKJV

Referring to religious people who would not bend to His authority, Jesus said that they "will be cast out into outer darkness. There will be weeping and gnashing of teeth."[364] There is the finality of hell's separation: "**There is a great gulf fixed.**" Hell fixes and finalizes all that separates a soul from God. Matthew warns us of the eternal consequences of going there and invites us to choose eternal life and enter the narrow gate, and he wrote:

> *"Then shall the King say unto them on his right hand, Come, ye blessed of my Father, inherit the kingdom prepared for you from the foundation of the world: ...Then shall he say also unto them on the left hand, Depart from me, ye cursed, into everlasting fire, prepared for the devil and his angels: And these shall go away into everlasting punishment: but the righteous into life eternal."*[365]

Mathew again admonished us:

> *"Enter through the narrow gate for wide is the gate and broad and easy to travel is the path that leads the way to destruction and eternal loss, and there are many who enter through it. But small is the gate and narrow and difficult to travel is the path that leads the way to everlasting life, and there are few who find it."*[366]

John warned:

> *"But the fearful, and unbelieving, and the abominable, and murderers, and whoremongers, and sorcerers, and idolaters, and all liars, shall have their part in the lake which burneth with fire and brimstone: which is the second death."*[367]

Yes, there is a hell to shun! The fact is indisputable, the flame is inescapable and the finality is irrevocable.

"Jesus Christ is your get-out-of-jail-free card."

God loves you and has a beautiful plan for your life. John expressed the depth of God's love when he wrote:

"For God so loved the world, that he gave his only begotten Son, that whosoever believeth in him should not perish, but have everlasting life. For God sent not his Son into the world to condemn the world; but that the world through him might be saved." [368]

Jesus told us:

"I am the door: by me, if any man enter in, he shall be saved and shall go in and out, and find pasture. The thief cometh not, but for to steal, and to kill, and to destroy: I am come that they might have life and that they might have it more abundantly." [369]

We must individually receive Jesus Christ as Saviour and Lord; then we can know and experience God's love and plan for our lives. John reminded us: "but as many as received Him to them He gave the right to become children of God, to those who believe in His name." [370] "We receive Jesus Christ through faith. "For by grace you have been saved through faith, and that not of yourselves; it is the gift of God, not of works, lest anyone should boast." [371] In summary, there is a hell to shun. Do not choose to go there. Hell is a place of a) unquenchable fire; b) memory and remorse; c) thirst; d) misery and pain (Revelation 14:10-11, KJV); e) frustration and anger (Matthew 13:42,51, KJV); f) separation; (Revelation 2:11, KJV), and undiluted divine wrath (Revelation14:10, KJV). It was not prepared for you. Remember God loves you and has a wonderful plan for life, and His love can lift you up so you can sing with me this song:

Love Lifted Me

I was sinking deep in sin, far from the peaceful shore,
Very deeply stained within, sinking to rise no more;
But the Master of the sea heard my despairing cry,
From the waters lifted me, now safe am I.

Love lifted me! Love lifted me!
When nothing else could help, Love lifted me.
Love lifted me! Love lifted me!
When nothing else could help, Love lifted me.

All my heart to Him I give, ever to Him, I'll cling,
In His blessed presence live, ever His praises sing.
Love so mighty and so true merits my soul's best songs;
Faithful, loving service, too, to Him belongs.

Souls in danger, look above, **Jesus** completely saves;
He will lift you by His love out of the angry waves.
He's the Master of the sea, billows His will obey;
He your Saviour wants to be, be saved today.

James Rowe (1865-1933)

PART 3

THE NEW JERUSALEM

"And I John saw the holy city, new Jerusalem, coming down from God out of heaven, prepared as a bride adorned for her husband"[372] *(Revelation 21:2, KJV). "And he carried me away in **the** Spirit to a great and high mountain, and showed me **the** great **city**, **the holy Jerusalem**, descending out of heaven from God."*

-REVELATION 21:10, KJV

CHAPTER FOURTEEN

THE NEW JERUSALEM –
THE HOLY CITY

"But ye are come unto mount Zion, and unto the city of the living God, the heavenly Jerusalem, and to an innumerable company of angels. "[373]

-HEBREWS 12:22, KJV

There exists a holy city called the new Jerusalem. It has twelve gates, *and* each gate is made of one pearl. This beautiful and blessed city is not only the centre of God's presence, but will be the permanent home for all the redeemed throughout eternity. Both Old and New Testaments believers looked and longed for this celestial city, as expressed in the following Scriptures:

▶ "There is a river; the streams of which shall make glad the city of God, the holy place of the tabernacles of the Most High."[374]

▶ "Glorious things are spoken of thee, O city of God. Selah."[375]

> "For he looked for a city which hath foundations, whose builder and maker is God. But now they desire a better country, that is, a heavenly: wherefore God is not ashamed to be called their God."[376]

> "In my Father's house are many mansions: if it were not so, I would have told you. I go to prepare a place for you. And if I go and prepare a place for you, I will come again and receive you unto myself; that where I am, there ye may also be."[377]

The new Jerusalem **is a literal city**. It has gold, streets, dimensions, stones, and in this new home of the church, all the materials are provided by God. **It is a heavenly city** that comes down out of heaven. "But now they desire a better country, that is, a heavenly; wherefore God is not ashamed to be called their God, for He hath prepared for them a city."[378] **It is a home city**. John described it to be the eternal home of Christians, whose glorified bodies will correspond to Christ's. Others, of course, will also share this glory.[379]

It is a vast city. The shape of this city is "four-square, and the length is as large as the breadth …the length and the breadth and the height of it are equal."[380] This description allows for two possibilities, namely, that the new Jerusalem is either in the shape of a cube or of a *vast* pyramid. The size of this city: "…and he measured the city with the reed, twelve thousand furlongs."[381] According to our present-day measurements, this city would be roughly 1,400 miles long, high and wide. Our earth has approximately 120 million square miles of water surface and 60 million square miles of land surface. If one multiplies 1,400 by 1,400 by 1,400 (the dimensions of the new Jerusalem), you arrive at the total cubic miles of the city, a figure of two billion, 700 million. This is some fifteen times the combined surface of the entire earth, including both land and water area.

It is a glorious city. The glory of God is to be its light: "having the glory of God; and her light was like unto a stone most precious, even like a jasper stone, clear as crystal."[382] The Lamb is the source of all necessary illumination. There will be no need of natural lights.

It is a capital city. God's eternal home is to be in this capital city of the new Jerusalem, which is the centre of divine presence and government in the universe of God and the Lamb. John saw the holy city, new Jerusalem, coming down from God out of heaven, prepared as a bride adorned for her husband.[383] He heard a great voice out of heaven saying, behold, the tabernacle of God is with men, and he will dwell with them, and they shall be his people, and God himself shall be with them, and be their God,[384] and God shall wipe away all tears from their eyes; and there shall be no more death, neither sorrow, nor crying, neither shall there be any more pain: for the former things are passed away.[385]

John was carried away in the spirit to a great and high mountain, and was shown that great city, the holy Jerusalem, descending out of heaven from God, having the glory of God: and her light was like unto a stone most precious, even like a jasper stone, clear as crystal.[386] The wall of the city had twelve foundations, and on them were the names of the twelve apostles of the Lamb.

"And he who talked with me had a gold reed to measure the city, its gates, and its wall."[387] The construction of its wall was *of* **jasper**; and the city *was* **pure gold**, like clear glass.[388] The foundations of the wall of the **city** *were* **adorned with all kinds of precious stones**: the first foundation *was* **jasper**, the second **sapphire**, the third **chalcedony**, the fourth **emerald**, the fifth **sardonyx**, the sixth **sardius**, the seventh **chrysolite**, the eighth **beryl**, the ninth **topaz**, the tenth **chrysoprase**, the eleventh **jacinth** and the twelfth **amethyst**."[389]

The **twelve gates** *were* **twelve pearls**: each gate was of one pearl, and the street of the city *was* pure gold, like transparent glass.[390] There was no temple in the city, "for the Lord God Almighty and the Lamb are its temple. The city had no need of the sun or the moon to shine in it, for the glory of God illuminated it. The Lamb *is* its light."[391]

The Inhabitants of this City

The holy and elect angels: "But ye come unto mount Sion and unto the city of the living God, the heavenly Jerusalem, and to an innumerable company of angels."[392] "And I beheld, and one heard the voice of many angels round about the throne, and the beasts, and the elders: and the number of them was ten thousand times ten thousand, and thousands of thousands."[393] God, of course, knows their number, but they are presented to men as uncountable.

The Father: "And immediately I was in the spirit; and, behold, a throne was set in heaven, and one sat on the throne. And he that sat was to look upon like a jasper and a sardine stone: and there was a rainbow round about the throne, in sight like unto an emerald."[394]

The Son: "And I beheld, and, lo, in the midst of the throne and of the four beasts, and in the midst of the elders, stood a Lamb as it had been slain, having seven horns and seven eyes, which are the seven Spirits of God sent forth into all the earth."[395]

The Holy Spirit: "And I heard a voice from heaven saying unto me, Write, Blessed are the dead which die in the Lord from henceforth: Yea, saith the Spirit, that they may rest from their labours: and their works do follow them."[396]

The Church: "But ye come unto mount Sion, and unto the city of the living God, the heavenly Jerusalem, and to an innumerable company of angels, to the general assembly and church of the firstborn, which are written in heaven, and the God the Judge of all, and to the spirits of just men made perfect."[397]

"And after these things I heard a great voice of much people in heaven, saying, Alleluia; salvation, and glory, and honour, and power, unto the Lord our God. But there shall by no means enter it anything that defiles, or causes an abomination or a lie, but only those who are written in the Lamb's book of life."[398]

"Him that overcomes will I make a pillar in the temple of my God, and he shall go no more out: and I will write upon him the name of my God, and the name of the city of my God, which is new Jerusalem, which cometh down out of heaven from my God: and I will write upon him my **new** name."[399] So, when we reach the tenth gate, the Inspection Gate, and we stand before God at the judgement, God will say to us, "**Well done thou good and faithful servants**, enter the new Jerusalem with all its splendour and glory." The new Jerusalem will be an exciting city. It will be a place of singing. The apostle John during his vision of the Revelation declares:

"And they sang a new song, saying: You are worthy to take the scroll and to open its seals; for You were slain, and have redeemed us to God by Your blood out of every tribe and tongue and people and nation" (Revelation 5:9, NKJV). "And they sing the song of Moses the servant of God, and the song of the Lamb, saying, Great and marvellous are thy works, Lord God Almighty; just and true are thy ways, thou King of saints."

-REVELATION. 15:3, KJV

The new Jerusalem will be a place where real and eternal fellowship will prevail. Not only will Christians enjoy blessed fellowship with other believers, but, even more important, we shall know and be known by the Saviour in a far more intimate way than ever possible here on earth. The Apostle Paul reminds us that: "For now we see through a glass, darkly; but then face to face: now I know in part; but then shall I know even as also I am known" (1 Corinthians 13:12, KJV).

The new Jerusalem will be a place of serving. The apostle John again declares:

"Therefore, are they before the throne of God, and serve him day and night in his temple: and he that sitteth on the throne shall dwell among them."

-REVELATION 7:15, KJV

95

"And there shall be no more curse: but the throne of God and of the Lamb shall be in it; and his servants shall serve him."

-REVELATION 22:3, KJV

"And there shall be no night there, and they need no candle, neither light of the sun; for the Lord God giveth them light: and they shall reign forever and ever."

-REVELATION 22:5, KJV

The new Jerusalem will be a place of learning.

"For we know in part, and we prophesy in part. But when that which is perfect is come, then that which is in part shall be done away."

-1 CORINTHIANS 13:9,10, KJV

In that city of eternal glory, we will learn concerning: a) the person of God; b) the Plan of God, and c) the Power of God. Indeed, we will also learn about "the riches of His glory" (Ephesians 3:16, KJV); "the **riches** of the **glory** of His **in**heritance **in** the saints (Ephesians 1:18, KJV), and "His riches in glory by Christ Jesus" (Philippians 4:19, KJV).

My longing is that the awesomeness of the new Jerusalem will renew your strength, courage and hope. It is there in the new Jerusalem you will see Jesus face to face and the many heroes of our faith. You will meet your loved ones who died in the Lord. You will bow on your knees before God and cry "Holy, holy, holy LORD God Almighty." You will clap your hands and sing "Glory, glory, glory to the Son of God." Let the hymns below be your songs of praises as you prepare to be among the many believers in Jesus Christ who will be sweeping through the twelve gates of the new Jerusalem. May the poems 'Jerusalem the City of God' and 'Jerusalem Praise' enrich your witness.

Who, Who Are These Beside the Chilly Wave

1. Who, who are these beside the chilly wave,
   Just on the borders of the silent grave,
   Shouting Jesus' power to save,
   "Washed in the blood of the Lamb"?

Refrain

"Sweeping through the gates" of the new Jerusalem,
"Washed in the blood of the Lamb,"
"Sweeping through the gates" of the new Jerusalem,
"Washed in the blood of the Lamb."

2. These, these are they who, in their youthful days,
   Found Jesus early, and in wisdom's ways
   Proved the fullness of His grace,
   "Washed in the blood of the Lamb."

3. These, these are they who, in affliction's woes,
   Ever have found in Jesus calm repose,
   Such as from a pure heart flows,
   "Washed in the blood of the Lamb."

4. Safe, safe upon the ever shining shore,
   Sin, pain, and death, and sorrow are all o'er;
   Happy now and evermore,
   "Washed in the blood of the Lamb."

Tullius C. O'Kane (1830-1912)

The Holy City

Last night I lay a-sleeping
There came a dream so fair,
I stood in old Jerusalem
Beside the temple there.

I heard the children singing,
And ever as they sang,
Me thought the voice of angels
From heaven in answer rang
Me thought the voice of angels
From heaven in answer rang.

Jerusalem! Jerusalem!
Lift up your gates and sing,
Hosanna in the highest!
Hosanna to your King!

And then me thought my dream was changed,
The streets no longer rang,
Hushed were the glad Hosannas
The little children sang.

The sun grew dark with mystery,
The morn was cold and chill,
As the shadow of a cross arose
Upon a lonely hill.

Jerusalem! Jerusalem!
Hark! How the angels sing,
Hosanna in the highest!
Hosanna to your King!

And once again the scene was changed;
New earth there seemed to be;
I saw the Holy City
Beside the tideless sea.

The light of God was on it's streets,
The gates were open wide,
And all who would might enter,
And no one was denied.

No need of moon or stars by night,
Or sun to shine by day;
It was the new Jerusalem
That would not pass away.

Jerusalem! Jerusalem!
Sing for the night is o'er!
Hosanna in the highest!
Hosanna for evermore

Frederick Edward Weatherly (1848-1929)

Jerusalem The City Of God

Jerusalem is called the city of our LORD.
The LORD has put His name there.
Jerusalem shall be called the faithful city.
The LORD has put His name there.
Jerusalem is called the mountain of the LORD of hosts.
The LORD has put His name there.
Jerusalem shall be called the holy mountain.
The LORD has put His name there.
Jerusalem shall be called the Throne of the LORD.
The LORD has put His name there.
The LORD dwells in Jerusalem,
All nations shall gather in the presence of the LORD in Jerusalem,

Kenrick H. Burgess

Jerusalem Praise

Praise the LORD, O Jerusalem!
He has comforted His people.
Praise the LORD, O Jerusalem!
He has taken away His judgments against you.
Praise the LORD, O Jerusalem!
He has cleared away your enemies.
Praise the LORD, O Jerusalem!
He is in your midst.
Praise the LORD, O Jerusalem!
You will fear disaster no more.
Praise the LORD, O Jerusalem!
He has redeemed Jerusalem.
Praise the LORD who dwells in Jerusalem!
Rejoice for Jerusalem! and be glad for her.

Kenrick H. Burgess

CHAPTER FIFTEEN

OLD CITY TO NEW CITY

"Blessed is every one who fears the Lord, who walks in His ways."
-PSALM 128:1, NKJV

What a journey, walking in Jerusalem and examining its gates. The city of Jerusalem had its years of wars, battles and destructions. It is a miracle that the city of Jerusalem is here with us today and is still at centre stage, and the wars continue. When will they cease? What is amazing is the unconditional love that God has for Jerusalem. The old Jerusalem was a shadow or symbolic earthly city of the incomparable new Jerusalem, which is in the heaven of heavens, where those who are redeemed by the blood of Jesus and are saved by grace will be forever with our Lord Jesus Christ. It is the eternal city of eternal righteousness and eternal peace. God built it.

The entry and exit gates in the of Jerusalem in Nehemiah's day represented the expedition of the Christian to the new Jerusalem. Jerusalem was where Jesus was circumcised in the Jewish temple eight days after His birth and presented before the LORD. When Jesus was twelve years old, He impressed the sages at the Jewish temple. Jesus recognized a widow's contribution of a mite in the temple which was all that she had and cited her offering as an example of giving. He taught the people in the temple courts. Jesus walked on the streets of Jerusalem. He restored a blind man's eyesight at the pool of Siloam.

There in Jerusalem by the Sheep Gate at Bethesda He healed a certain man who had an infirmity thirty-eight years on the Sabbath day. On another Sabbath day, He entered the synagogue and taught, and healed a man whose right hand was withered. In Jerusalem, He appointed twelve disciples and sent them out to preach, heal sicknesses and to cast out demons. He also went up on a mountain and taught them the Beatitudes. He healed the servant of a Roman centurion who was lying at home paralyzed and dreadfully tormented because of the centurion's great faith.

Mary poured oil on His head and anointed His feet there. One day He entered Jerusalem riding triumphantly on a young donkey, and the people sang praises unto him. He taught the people there. He spent the last days of His ministry in Jerusalem. He washed the feet of His disciples there. In Jerusalem, He held His last supper and sang a hymn with the disciples.

In the garden of Gethsemane, He prayed with great agony. He was betrayed by one of His disciples with a kiss and healed and restored a soldier's ear that was cut-off when he came to arrest Him. He was interrogated by the high priest, Caiaphas, the Sanhedrin, the governor Pilate and He was mocked by King Herod. Pilate found no fault in Him yet he sentenced Him to be crucified in response to the shouts of the people to crucify Him. There on a cross on the hill called Calvary which was approximately six miles from Bethlehem where He was born, Jesus was crucified and died. His body was buried and sealed in another's tomb, but on the third day, He arose victoriously from the dead. He instructed His disciples to wait in Jerusalem until they were endued with power from on high, then He was taken up into heaven from there. His disciples were filled with the Holy Spirit in Jerusalem, and the early church was born there.

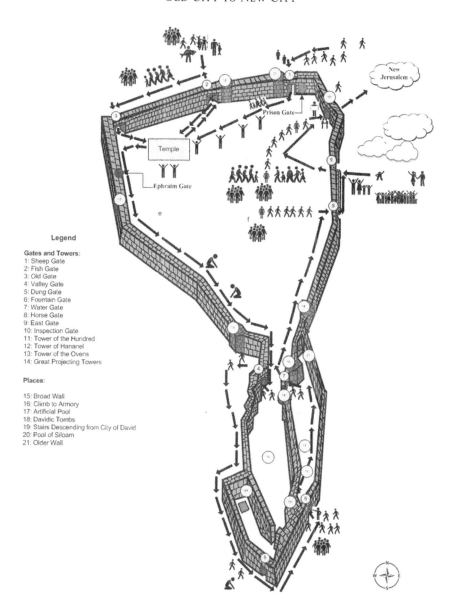

Figure 2: Burgess illustration of the Christian Walk through the gates of Jerusalem

Figure 2 above shows an illustration (not to scale) of the Christian's walk through the gates in the old Jerusalem on their way to the New Jerusalem. Jesus said, I am the door of the sheep, by me if anyone enters, he shall go in and out and find pasture. I am the good shepherd: the good shepherd gives his life for the sheep.

We, like sheep, entered the **Sheep Gate**, where we received Jesus as our Lord and Saviour. His Holy Spirit took residence within us, and our bodies became the temple in which He lives, and we were then called Christians. We received a new life. We were then taught at the temple (local church) and developed a personal, daily relationship with Jesus and became disciples of Jesus who said:

> "By this is my Father is glorified, that you bear much fruit; so, you will be my disciples."
>
> -JOHN 15:8, KJV

The second gate, the **Fish Gate**, was where we were taught to be fishers of men and obeyed the command of Jesus to *"go and make disciples of all nations, baptizing them in the name of the Father and of the Son and the Holy Spirit, and teaching them to obey everything I have commanded you."*[400] The Fish Gate is symbolic of evangelism, where we reach out to men, women and children and share the good news of salvation with them so that they, too, can be saved and delivered from the power and control of sin. We also invite them into the temple for worship. It is there they will be fed and encouraged to follow Jesus, who is the way, the truth and the life. The third gate, the **Old Gate**, was a picture of our sanctification and continuous walk in holiness without which no man can see God.

It is the place where we can worship, saying, "Holy, holy, holy, Lord God Almighty, Who was and is and is to come!" We then cast our crowns before His throne, singing,

"Thou art worthy, O Lord, to receive glory and honour and power: for Thou hast created all things, and for Thy pleasure, they are and were created."

-REVELATION 4:11, KJV

At the Old Gate, you must dare to be a Joseph: He succeeded, not in himself but really in and through Christ, of whom he was a type. Like Christ, he maintained flawlessness of character. Sold like his Lord, like Christ, he also manifested faithfulness to those who betrayed him. Like Christ, he modelled fruitfulness in physically saving the world. Note also the fourfold expression, "the Lord was with Joseph."[401] Note further the twofold expression, "The Lord made all he did to prosper."[402] Then the person, presence and power of God in Christ in and with Joseph and us is the fundamental secret of superior spiritual standing. So then, just you be Christ's Joseph, just stand up, stand down, just stand in and fear no frown, just you gain God's crown!

It is this holy life that carried us to and through the fourth gate, the **Valley Gate**, with its trials, difficulties and troubles that came our way and strengthens us who walk by faith. In the valley, we sometimes seemed to be alone, but Jesus was always with us. The Lord is our Shepherd in the valley.

Hence the reason why James encouraged us to count it all joy when we fall into various kinds of temptations, because we know that the trial of our faith produces patience, and if we allow patience to do its work we shall be perfect and entirely lacking nothing.

In the valley you must make every effort to add to your faith goodness; and to goodness, knowledge; and to knowledge, self-control; and to self-control, perseverance; and to perseverance, godliness; and to godliness, mutual affection; and to mutual affection, love. If you possess these qualities in increasing measure, they will keep you from being ineffective and unproductive in your knowledge of our Lord Jesus Christ. But whoever does not have them is nearsighted and blind, forgetting that they have been cleansed from their past sins.

Therefore, you must make every effort to confirm your calling and election. For if you do these things, you will never stumble, and you will receive a rich welcome into the eternal kingdom of our Lord and Saviour Jesus Christ.[403]

The fifth gate, the **Dung Gate**, is critical. There, you must eliminate the impediments that would hinder you from running the race to win "gold." Like Paul, "...this one thing you must do, forgetting those things which are behind, and reaching forth unto those things which are before, you must press toward the mark for the prize of the high calling of God in Christ Jesus."[404]

There must be mental elimination. You cannot win the gold if your mind is cluttered with worldly things, values and pleasures. You must keep your eyes on Jesus. Concentration is a must. One thing is important, as the apostle Paul declared, "that I may know Christ, and the power of his resurrection, and the fellowship of his sufferings being made conformable unto his death."[405] There must be a transformation. You must renew your mind and put on the mind of Christ.[406]

There must also be moral elimination: Paul guided us when he said, "....what things were gain to me, those I counted loss for Christ. Yea doubtless, and I count all things but loss for the excellency of the knowledge of Christ Jesus my Lord: for whom I have suffered the loss of all things, and do count them but **dung**, that I may win Christ, and be found in him, not having my own righteousness."[407] Also, he continued, "let us walk by the same rule, let us mind the same thing."[408]

Remember, we have the same Saviour, Jesus Christ, and only one standard, the Word of God – the Bible. At the Dung Gate, sins must be forgiven; past successes must be forgotten and self-righteousness (that is self in control of your life instead of God) must be forbidden. Let us continue the race before us and turn the corner along the eastern wall.

The **Fountain Gate** is the sixth gate. It is where you are filled with the Holy Spirit, and receive from Him love, joy, peace, patience, gentleness, goodness, faith, meekness, temperance and power for living so that you can receive power for living and to overcome spiritual warfare.

The Holy Spirit must be your comforter, guide and director. He must have all of you. Remember, your body is a temple of the Holy Spirit. Do not grieve Him for your victory comes not by might, nor by your power, but by the Holy Spirit.

The **seventh gate**, the **Water Gate**, is where we continue to learn and hide in our hearts the Word of God. We are admonished to take up the sword of the Holy Spirit, which is the Word of God, for spiritual warfare at the **Horse Gate**. The Word of God becomes alive to each of us, allowing cleansing and encouragement to fight the good fight of faith so that we could finish our race on earth. The eighth gate in our journey, the **Horse Gate**, is a symbol of the spiritual warfare that we must pass through. We must put on the overall armour of God and keep the faith, singing this beautiful hymn by Francis Rous (1579–1659), "**The Lord Is My Shepherd**."

The Lord is my Shepherd

1. The Lord's my Shepherd, I'll not want;
   He makes me down to lie
   In pastures green; He leadeth me
   The quiet waters by.

2. My soul, He doth restore again,
   And me to walk doth make
   Within the paths of righteousness,
   E'en for His own name's sake.

3. Yea, though I walk in death's dark vale,
   Yet will I fear no ill;
   For Thou art with me, and Thy rod
   And staff my comfort still.

4. My table Thou hast furnished me
    In the presence of my foes;
    My head Thou dost with oil anoint,
    And my cup overflows.

5. Goodness and mercy all my life
    Shall surely follow me;
    And in God's house forevermore,
    My dwelling place shall be.

We must keep our eyes on Jesus, never looking back at our inheritance at the Ephraim Gate that we passed on our way to the Valley Gate. We must be encouraged by the following words of the apostle Peter:

*"Blessed be the God and Father of our Lord Jesus Christ, who according to His abundant mercy has begotten us again to a living hope through the resurrection of Jesus Christ from the dead, **to an inheritance incorruptible and undefiled and that does not fade away, reserved in heaven for you**, who are kept by the power of God through faith for salvation ready to be revealed in the last time."*[409]

-1 PETER 1:3–5, KJV

We must keep looking up for the appearing of our Lord Jesus Christ in the air. We must always remember that God will give us grace and more grace. We can encourage ourselves in the Lord by singing my favourite hymn by **Annie J. Flint (1866–1932)**.

He Giveth More Grace

1. He giveth more grace as our burdens grow greater,
    He sendeth more strength as our labours increase;
    To added afflictions He addeth His mercy,
    To multiplied trials, He multiplies peace.

Chorus

His love has no limits; His grace has no measure,
His power no boundary known unto men;
For out of His infinite riches in Jesus
He giveth, and giveth, and giveth again.

2. When we have exhausted our store of endurance,
   When our strength has failed ere the day is half done,
   When we reach the end of our hoarded resources
   Our Father's full giving is only begun.

(Chorus)

At the ninth gate, the **East Gate**, we are strengthened by the apostle Paul when he declared:

"Behold I shew you a mystery; We shall not all sleep, **but we shall all be changed, in a moment, in the twinkling of an eye, at the last trump: for the trumpet shall sound, and the dead shall be raised incorruptible, and we shall be changed.**

For this corruptible must put on incorruption, and this mortal must put on immortality. So, when this corruptible shall have put on incorruption, and this mortal shall have put on immortality, then shall be brought to pass the saying that is written, Death is swallowed up in the victory. O death, where is thy sting? O grave, where is thy victory? The sting of death is sin; and the strength of sin is the law, **but thanks be to God, who gave us the victory through our Lord Jesus Christ.** *Therefore, my beloved brethren, be ye steadfast, unmovable, always abounding in the work of the Lord, forasmuch as ye know that your labour is not in vain in the Lord."*[410]

-1 CORINTHIANS 15:51–58, KJV

So when you reach the tenth gate, the **Inspection Gate**, you would have shunned the **Prison Gate**, bubbling over with the joy of your salvation, and as you stand before God at the judgment, He will say to you, **"Well-done thou good and faithful servant,** enter the **new Jerusalem and enjoy all its magnificence and glory!**

Now that you have completed your walk through the gates of Jerusalem, you can lift holy hands and praise the God of heaven, thanking Him for the things that He has taught you. I trust that you have discovered your God-ordained destiny and purpose. Sing with boldness the beautiful hymn of praise and worship **'All Hail the Power of Jesus Name.'**

All Hail the Power of Jesus' Name

1. *All hail the power of Jesus' name!*
   Let angels prostrate fall;
   bring forth the royal diadem,
   and crown him Lord of all.
   Bring forth the royal diadem
   and crown him Lord of all.

2. *Ye chosen seed of Israel's race,*
   ye ransomed from the fall,
   hail him who saves you by his grace,
   and crown him Lord of all
   Hail him who saves you by his grace,
   and crown him Lord of all.

3. *Sinners, whose love can ne'er forget*
   the wormwood and the gall,
   go spread your trophies at his feet and crown him Lord of all.
   Go spread your trophies at his feet,
   and crown him Lord of all.

110

4. *Let every kindred, every tribe*
   on this terrestrial ball,
   to him all majesty ascribe,
   and crown him Lord of all.
   To him, all majesty ascribe and crown him Lord of all.

5. *O that with yonder sacred throng*
   we at his feet may fall!
   We'll join the everlasting song,
   and crown him Lord of all.
   We'll join the everlasting song
   and crown him Lord of all.

Let us join and sing the **Hallelujah Chorus** from Handel's "Messiah."

Hallelujah Chorus from "Messiah"
Hallelujah hallelujah hallelujah hallelujah hallelujah
Hallelujah hallelujah hallelujah hallelujah hallelujah
For the Lord God Omnipotent reigneth
Hallelujah hallelujah hallelujah hallelujah
For the Lord God Omnipotent reigneth
Hallelujah hallelujah hallelujah hallelujah
For the Lord God Omnipotent reigneth
Hallelujah hallelujah hallelujah hallelujah
Hallelujah hallelujah hallelujah hallelujah
Hallelujah hallelujah hallelujah hallelujah
(For the Lord God Omnipotent reigneth)
Hallelujah hallelujah hallelujah hallelujah
For the Lord God Omnipotent reigneth
(Hallelujah hallelujah hallelujah hallelujah)
Hallelujah

The kingdom of this world;
is become the kingdom of our Lord,
and of His Christ, and of His Christ
And He shall reign forever and ever
And He shall reign forever and ever
And He shall reign forever and ever
And He shall reign forever and ever

King of kings forever and ever hallelujah hallelujah
and Lord of lords forever and ever hallelujah hallelujah
King of kings forever and ever hallelujah hallelujah
and Lord of lords forever and ever hallelujah hallelujah
King of kings forever and ever hallelujah hallelujah
and Lord of lords.
King of kings and lord of lords
And He shall reign, And He shall reign, And He shall reign
He shall reign, And He shall reign forever and ever

King of kings forever and ever
and Lord of lords hallelujah hallelujah
And He shall reign forever and ever
King of kings and Lord of lords
King of kings and Lord of lords
And He shall reign forever and ever
Forever and ever and ever and ever
(King of kings and Lord of lords)
Hallelujah hallelujah hallelujah hallelujah
Hallelujah.

George Frideric Handel (1685–1759)

My Praise

I praise God with the words of the apostle Peter who wrote:

"Blessed be the God and Father of our Lord Jesus Christ, who according to His abundant mercy has begotten us again to a living hope through the resurrection of Jesus Christ from the dead, to an inheritance incorruptible and undefiled and that does not fade away, reserved in heaven for you, who are kept by the power of God through faith for salvation ready to be revealed in the last time."

-1 PETER 1: 5, NKJV

My Prayer

I thank You, Lord, for giving me the inspiration, strength and joy to write this book. I am humbled by the wisdom, patience, love, anointings, favour, and guidance bestowed on me during this book journey. It is my prayer that everyone who reads this book will be blessed. I ask that the presence of the Holy Spirit be in the house or place where ever this book is lodged, in every continent on planet earth. This is my prayer. Continue to bless Jerusalem with Your presence. I am overwhelmed by Your love towards me. I cannot understand it, but this one thing I know, I will serve You, LORD, as You give me breath. All the glory of this book belongs to You Elohim. Grant your servant favour. I Thank You, Lord, Amen.

In Closing

I urge you who do not have a personal relationship Jesus Christ re-visit the Sheep Gate and turn to Him today. This gate is open to all. Wherever you are, whoever, you are, you can receive Jesus Christ as your Lord and Saviour. I want you to remember that:

1) You need salvation (Romans 3: 23, KJV).

2) Jesus died for your sins (Romans 5:8, KJV).

3) Salvation is a gift of God (Romans 6:23).

4) You are saved by grace through faith, and not of yourself (Ephesians 2: 8-9, KJV).

5) God saves all who call upon Him (Romans10:13, KJV).

You can turn to God now and put your faith in Jesus Christ who died for you.

"If you confess with your mouth the Lord Jesus and believe in your heart that God has raised Him from the dead, you will be saved. For with the heart one believes unto righteousness, and with the mouth, confession is made unto salvation" (Romans 10:9-10, NKJV). Pray this simple prayer right now:

Dear Lord Jesus, I believe you are the Son of God and the only way to God. I believe that you died on the cross for my sins and rose again so that I might be forgiven and receive eternal life. I confess my sinfulness before You. I repent of my sins, I accept Your sacrifice on my behalf, and I ask you for forgiveness and the gift of eternal life. I now accept you as my Lord and Saviour.

Thank You! Amen

Congratulations! Welcome to the family of God.

ENDNOTES

[1]   Psalm 132:13–14, NKJV

[2]   Isaiah 4:3, NKJV

[3]   Jeremiah 3:17, NKJV

[4]   Zechariah 8:3, NKJV

[5]   Psalm 87:1–2, NKJV

[6]   Isaiah 52:1, NKJV

[7]   Zachariah 8:2–3, NKJV

Chapter 1

[8]   2 Chronicles 33:4b, NKJV

[9]   Genesis 14:17–20, KJV

[10]   1 Kings 5:1, KJV

[11]   Daniel 5, KJV

[12]   Ezra 7:1, 8, Neh. 2:1, KJV

[13]   Psalm 48:1, 8, KJV

[14]   Isaiah 60:14, NKJV

[15]   Joel 3:21, NKJV

[16]   Ps 132:13–14, NKJV

[17]   Isaiah 4:3, NKJV

[18]   Jeremiah 3:17, NKJV

[19]   Zechariah 8:3, NKJV

[20]   Psalm 132:13–14, KJV

21 Zechariah 8:3, NKJV

22 Psalm 87:1–3, NKJV

23 Psalm 125:2, NKJV

24 Ezekiel 37:7–11; 21–23, KJV

25 Joel 3:1–2, KJV

26 Luke 21:24, KJV

27 Nehemiah 1–2, KJV

28 Nehemiah 3–7, KJV

29 Psalm 122:2, NKJV

30 Isaiah 26:2, NKJV

31 Psalm 100:4–5, NKJV

32 John 10:9, KJV

33 Psalm 24:7–10, KJV

Chapter 2

34 Acts 16:31, NKJV

35 Nehemiah 3:1, 32, KJV

36 Isaiah 53:7, KJV

37 John 1:29, NKJV

38 Isaiah 53:6, KJV

39 Luke 19:10, KJV

40 Isaiah 53:6, KJV

41 Romans 5:8, NKJV

42 John 3:16, NKJV

43 John 10:9, KJV

44 John 10:7, NKJV

45 Colossians 2:13–14, KJV

46 John 1:12, KJV; Romans 8:15, KJV

47 John 5:24, KJV

48 Colossians 1:13–14, KJV

49 Colossians 1:27, KJV; Revelation 3:20, KJV

50 2 Corinthians 5:1, NKJV

51 2 Corinthians 5:21, KJV

52   1 John 4:9–11, KJV

53   Colossians 1:19–22, KJV

Chapter 3

54   Mark 16:15, KJV

55   Mathew 4:18–20, KJV

56   Luke 10:2–3, NIV

57   Mathew 28:19–20, NIV

58   John 21:17, NIV

59   Mathew 28:18–20, KJV

60   1 Thessalonians 2:19–20, KJV

61   Proverbs 11:30, KJV

62   James 5:20, KJV

63   Luke 15:10, KJV

64   Daniel 12:3

65   2 Corinthians 3:2, KJV; Galatians 2:20, KJV

66   Acts 1:8, KJV

67   1 Corinthians 15:58, KJV

Chapter 4

68   1 Peter 1:15, NKJV

69   Hebrews 12:14, NKJV

70   Nehemiah 3:6, KJV

71   2 Kings14:13, KJV; Jeremiah 31:38, KJV

72   Nehemiah 3:6, KJV

73   Nehemiah 12:39, KJV

74   Exodus 3:4–6a; 10, NKJV

75   1 Peter 1:14–16, NIV

76   Leviticus 19:2, NKJV

77   Leviticus 20:26, NKJV

78   Hebrews 12:14, KJV

79   1 Thessalonians 4:3–8, KJV

80   1 Peter 2:9, KJV

[81] Revelation 22:11, KJV

[82] Romans 12:1–2, KJV

[83] 1 Thess. 4: 3–8, NKJV

[84] Jeremiah 6:16, NIV

[85] Isaiah 63:11, KJV

[86] cf. Gen. 30:22–24, KJV

[87] cf. Gen. 39:8–9a, KJV

[88] Gen. 39:9, KJV

[89] cf. Psa. 51:4a; Gen. 39:9c, KJV

[90] 1 Corinthians 10:13, NIV

[91] Matthew 5:8, KJV

[92] John 8:12, NIV

[93] Proverbs 4:18, KJV

Chapter 5

[94] James 1:2–4, KJV

[95] James 1:2–4, 12, KJV

[96] Nehemiah 3:13, KJV

[97] 1 Thessalonians 3:3, KJV

[98] Acts 14:22, KJV

[99] Exodus 20:20, NIV

[100] Psalm 66:8–12, NIV

[101] 1 Peter 2:19–23, KJV

[102] 2 Timothy 3:12, KJV.

[103] 1 Peter 1:6–7, KJV

[104] 1 Peter 4:12–14, KJV

[105] Romans 5:3–5, KJV

[106] 2 Corinthians 1:3–5, KJV

[107] James 1:12, KJV

[108] Psalm 23, KJV

[109] Ezekiel 37:1–14, KJV

[110] Ezekiel 37:9, KJV

[111] Romans 4:17, KJV

112   Hebrews 4:12, NIV

113   1 Peter 1:23, KJV

114   John 6:63, KJV

115   Ephesians 2:1, KJV

116   Romans 3:12, KJV

117   Hebrews 4:12, NKJV

118   Isaiah 55:11, KJV

119   Mark 5:37, KJV

120   Mark 9:2, KJV

121   Philippians 3:10, KJV

122   2 Corinthians 5:21, KJV

123   Galatians 3:13, KJV

124   Mark 15:34, KJV

125   John 18:11, KJV

126   Nehemiah. 4:9, KJV; Mark 13:33, KJV; Eph. 6:18, KJV; Col. 4:2, KJV

127   John 16:32, KJV

128   Genesis 26:19, KJV

129   Deuteronomy 8:7, NKJV

Chapter 6

130   Ephesians 4:22-24, NKJV

131   Nehemiah 3:14, KJV

132   Exodus 29:14, KJV; Leviticus 4:11, KJV; 8:17, KJV; 16:27, KJV; Numbers 19:5, KJV

133   Ezekiel 4.12–15, KJV

134   Proverbs 4:24, NIV

135   James 3:16, KJV

136   Ephesians 4:22, 25, 27, 28–31, KJV

137   Galatians 5:16; 19–21, KJV

138   Romans 1:29–32, KJV

139   Ephesians 4:1, 2, KJV

140   Ephesians 4:17, 23, KJV

141   Ephesians 5:2, NKJV

142   Ephesians 5:8, 10, KJV

143   Hebrews 12:1–2, NKJV

144   2 Timothy 2:1–2, 4, 15–16, 21–22, KJV

Chapter 7

145   Ephesians 5:18–19, NKJV

146   Nehemiah 3:15, KJV

147   Nehemiah 3:15, KJV

148   Isaiah 8:6, KJV

149   2 Kings 20:20, KJV; 2 Chronicles 32:30, KJV

150   John 7:9, KJV

151   John 7:38, NIV

152   Romans 8:27, KJV

153   1 Corinthians 2:10, KJV

154   1 Corinthians 2:11, KJV

155   Acts 16:6–7, KJV

156   Acts 16:10, KJV

157   Acts 8:29, KJV

158   Acts 10:19, KJV

159   Acts 13:2, KJV

160   Revelation 2–3, KJV

161   Revelation 2:7, 11, 17, 29; 3:6, 13, 22, KJV

162   Romans 15:30, KJV

163   Ephesians 4:30, KJV

164   Romans 8:26, KJV

165   1 Corinthians 2:10–11, KJV

166   1 Corinthians 6:19, KJV

167   2 Corinthians 6:16, KJV

168   1 Corinthians 3:16, KJV

169   Romans 8:9, KJV

170   John 16:13, KJV

171   Hebrews 10:29, KJV

172   1 Peter 4:14, KJV

173 Romans 8:2, KJV

174 Ephesians 1:17, KJV

175 Acts 1:4, 5, KJV

176 Romans 8:15, KJV

177 Romans 1:4, KJV

178 2 Corinthians 4:13, KJV

179 John 14:26 KJV

180 John16:13–15, NKJV

181 Zechariah 4:6, KJV

182 Acts 1:8, KJV

183 Titus 3:5; John 3:3–7, KJV.

184 Romns 6:3,4; Gal. 3:3–27, KJV; Col. 2:12, KJV

185 John 14:20, KJV; 1 Cor. 3:16, KJV; John 7:37–39, KJV; Rom. 8:9, KJV; John 4:24, KJV

186 2 Cor. 1:22; Eph. 1:3, KJV

187 Acts 2:4, KJV

188 Romans 8:26, KJV; Jude 20, KJV; Ephesians 6:18, KJV

189 John 16:3, KJV; Romans 8:14, KJV

190 1 John 2:27, KJV

191 Acts 1:8, KJV

192 Romans 5:5, KJV

193 2 Corinthians 3:18, KJV

194 Ephesians 3:16, KJV

195 1 Corinthians 2:10, KJV

196 John 16:13–14, KJV

197 John 14:26, KJV

198 Romans 8:16, KJV; 1 John 3:24, KJV

199 2 Corinthians 3:17, KJV

200 Mark 13:11, KJV

201 Romans 8:26–27, KJV

202 Romans 12:6-8, KJV; 1 Peter 4:11, KJV; 1 Corinthians 12:4–11, KJV; Ephesians 4:11, KJV

203 Galatians 5:16–17, KJV

[204] Galatians 5:22–25, KJV

[205] Ephesians 5:18–20, KJV

[206] John 16:7, KJV

[207] Ephesians 4:22–32, KJV

[208] Ephesians 6:18, NIV

[209] Proverbs 3:4–8, NIV

Chapter 8

[210] Mathew 4:3, NIV

[211] Colossians 3:16a, KJV

[212] John 3:18, KJV

[213] Nehemiah 3:26, KJV

[214] Nehemiah 3:26, KJV

[215] Psalm 119:9, KJV

[216] John 15:3–4, KJV

[217] Hebrews 4:12, NKJV

[218] Deuteronomy 31:10–13, KJV

[219] Nehemiah 8:1–3, KJV

[220] 2 Samuel 22:31, KJV

[221] Psalm 12:6, KJV

[222] Psalm 119:9, KJV

[223] Psalm 147:15, KJV

[224] Deuteronomy 8:3, KJV

[225] Psalm 15:16, KJV

[226] 2 Timothy 2:16–17, KJV

[227] Psalm 19:10, KJV

[228] Psalm 19:8, KJV

[229] Psalm 119:105, KJV

[230] Proverbs 2:6, KJV

[231] Proverbs 6:23, KJV

[232] John 1:8, KJV

[233] Matthew 7:24, KJV

[234] Luke 11:28, KJV

235 John 8:31, KJV

236 John 15:3, KJV

237 John 17:7, KJV

238 1 Timothy 4:5, KJV

239 John 20:31, KJV

240 1 John 5:13, KJV

241 Isaiah 8:20, KJV

242 1 Thessalonians 2:13, KJV

243 Mathew 13:20, KJV

244 Revelation 22:19, KJV

245 Romans 10:17, KJV

246 Ephesians 6:17, KJV

247 Matthew 4:4, NKJV

248 Matthew 4:7, NKJV

249 Matthew 4:10–11, NKJV

250 2 Corinthians 10:3–5, KJV.

251 Psalm 19:7–11, KJV

Chapter 9

252 Ephesians 6:10–11, KJV

253 Nehemiah 3:28, KJV

254 2 Samuel. 5:7; 1 Chronicles 11:5, KJV

255 Romans 8:28, KJV

256 Revelation 19:11, NLT

257 Deuteronomy 20:1, KJV

258 Psalm 91:1–15, KJV

259 1 Peter 5:8, ESV

260 James 4:7, KJV

261 Deuteronomy 28:7, ESV

262 Isaiah 54:17, KJV

263 Romans 8:37, KJV

264 1 Corinthians 15:57, NKJV

265 2 Thessalonians 3:3, NIV

266 Ephesians 6: 10–18, KJV

267 Ephesians 6:10, KJV

268 Ephesians. 6:11, KJV

269 Ephesians 6:13, KJV

270 Ephesians 6:14, KJV

271 Romans 13:12, KJV

272 2 Corinthians. 6:7, KJV

273 Ephesians 6:14, KJV

274 Isaiah 11:5, KJV

275 1 Thessalonians 5:8, KJV

276 Ephesians 6:15, KJV

277 Ephesians. 6:16, KJV

278 Hebrews 11:1, KJV

279 Isaiah 12:2, KJV

280 Ephesians 6:17, KJV

281 2 Peter 3:18, KJV

282 Philippians 2:5, KJV

283 Romans 12:2, KJV

284 Nehemiah 4:9, KJV

285 Mark 13:33, KJV

286 Mark 14:38, KJV

287 Ephesians 6:18, KJV

288 Psalm 27:8, KJV

289 Psalm 46:1, KJV

Chapter 10

290 Matthew 24:42, 44, NKJV

291 Nehemiah 3:29, KJV

292 Ezekiel 47:1; 10:1–5,15–19, KJV

293 Ezekiel 43:1–5, KJV; Isaiah 6:1–4, KJV

294 Zechariah 9:9–10, KJV; Luke 19:29–49; 21:37–38, KJV; Ezekiel 44:1–2, KJV

295 Matthew 24:27; Zechariah 14:3, KJV

296 Matthew 24:1–3; Mark 13:1–4, KJV

297 Acts 1:12, KJV

298 Zechariah 14:4, KJV

299 Psalm 24, KJV

300 Ezekiel 44:1–2, KJV

301 1 Thessalonians 4:13–18, NKJV

302 John 14:1–3 and 1 Thessalonians 4:16, KJV

303 John 14:1–3, KJV

304 1Thessalonians 4:14–15, NKJV

305 1 Thessalonians 4:16, KJV

306 1 Corinthians 15:52, KJV

307 1 Thessalonians 4:16, KJV

308 1 Thessalonians 4:16, KJV

309 1 Thessalonians 4:16–17, KJV

310 1 Corinthians 15:51, 53, KJV

311 1 Thessalonians 4:17, KJV

312 1 Thessalonians 4:17, KJV

313 1 Thessalonians 4:17, KJV

314 John 14:3, NKJV

315 1 Thessalonians 4:17, KJV

316 2 Corinthians 5.10, KJV

317 Romans 14:10, KJV; 2 Corinthians 5:10, KJV

318 1 Corinthians 3:11–15, KJV

319 Matthew 24:21, KJV

320 1 John3:2–3, KJV

321 Matthew 24:45, KJV

322 Matthew 24:46–47, KJV

323 2 Timothy 4:8, KJV

324 Titus 2:11–13, NKJV

Chapter 11

325 Romans 14:10b, 12, KJV

326 Nehemiah 3:29, KJV

[327]   Psalm 39:4, KJV

[328]   Hebrews 9:27, KJV

[329]   Mathew 25:31–33, KJV

[330]   2 Peter 3:9, KJV

[331]   2 Peter 3:9, KJV

[332]   Matthew 13:44–46, NKJV

[333]   Luke 12:33–34, KJV

[334]   1 Timothy 6:18–19, KJV

[335]   2 Corinthians 5:10, KJV

[336]   Matthew 6:33, KJV

Chapter 12

[337]   Galatians 3:29, KJV

[338]   Nehemiah 8:16; 12:39, KJV

[339]   cf. Gen. 30:22–24, KJV

[340]   Genesis 48:10, KJV

[341]   Proverbs17:6, KJV

[342]   Genesis 48:1–2, KJV

[343]   Genesis 48:1, 8–11, KJV

[344]   Genesis 48:3, KJV

[345]   Genesis 48:15–16, KJV

[346]   Genesis 48:15, KJV

[347]   Genesis 48:17–20, KJV

[348]   1 Samuel 16:7, KJV

Chapter 13

[349]   John 3:17–18, NKJV

[350]   Nehemiah 12:39, KJV

[351]   Luke 16:19–31, NKJV

[352]   Luke 16:19, 22–24, KJV

[353]   Luke 16:28, KJV

[354]   Luke 16:24, KJV

355   Luke 16:25, NKJV

356   Luke 16:24, KJV

357   Luke 16:28, KJV

358   Romans 14:7, NKJV

359   Luke 16:25–26, KJV

360   Luke 16:25, KJV

361   Matthew 25:46, KJV

362   Matthew 10:28, NKJV

363   2 Thessalonians 1:7–10, NKJV

364   Matthew 8:12, NKJV

365   Matthew 25:34; 41, 46, KJV

366   Matthew 7:13–14, AMP

367   Revelation 21:8, KJV

368   John 3:16–17, KJV

369   John10:9–10, KJV

370   John 1:12, NKJV

371   Ephesians 2:8, 9, KJV

Chapter 14

372   Revelation 21:2, KJV

373   Heb. 12:22, NKJV

374   Psalm 46:4, KJV

375   Psalm 87:3, KJV

376   Heb. 11:10, 16, KJV

377   John 14:2, 3, KJV

378   Hebrews 11:16, KJV

379   Revelation 21:24–26, KJV

380   Rev. 21:16, KJV

381   Rev. 21:16, KJV

382   Revelation 21:11, KJV

383   Revelation 21:2, KJV

384   Revelation 21:3, KJV

385   Revelation 21:4, KJV

386 Revelation 21:10–11, KJV

387 Revelation 21:14–15, KJV

388 Revelation 21:18, KJV

389 Revelation 21:19–20, KJV

390 Revelation. 21:21, KJV

391 Revelation 21:22–23, KJV

392 Heb. 12:22, KJV

393 Revelation 5:11, KJV

394 Revelation 4:2,3, KJV

395 Revelation 5:6, KJV

396 Revelation 14:13, KJV

397 Hebrews 12:22, 23, KJV

398 Revelation 21:27, KJV

399 Revelation 3:12, KJV

Chapter 15

400 Matthew 28:19–20 NIV

401 Genesis 39:2, 3, 21, 23, KJV

402 Genesis 39:3, 23, KJV

403 2 Peter 1:10–11, NIV

404 Philippians 3:13–14, KJV

405 Philippians 3:10, NKJV

406 Romans 12:1–2, KJV

407 Philippians 3:7–9, KJV

408 Philippians 3:16

409 1 Peter 1:3–5, NKJV

410 1 Corinthians 15:51–58, KJV

REFERENCES

1. Dake, F.J. 1999. Dake's Annotated Reference Bible. Georgia, USA: Dake Publishing, Inc.

2. Henry, Matthew. 1991. Matthew Henry's Commentary. Peabody, Massachusetts : Hendrickson Publishers.

3. LaHaye, Tim and Jerry B. Jenkins 1999. Are we living in the End Times. Wheaton, Illinois: House Publishers, Inc.

4. Stone, N 1944. Names of God. Chicago: Moody Press

5. Wiersbe, W.W. 2007. The Wiersbe Bible Commentary. Colorado Springs : David C. Cook.

6. Willmington, H. L.1984. Willmington Guide to the Bible. Wheaton, Illinois:Tyndale House Publishers, Inc.

7. Central Bureau of Statistics, 2013. Statistics Report. Israel : Ministry of Tourism.